Life *After* Suicide

Survival, Hope, and Healing

Cynthia L. Long

CSS Publishing Company, Inc.
Lima, Ohio

LIFE AFTER SUICIDE

FIRST EDITION
Copyright © 2011
by CSS Publishing Co., Inc.

Scripture quotations are from the New Revised Standard Version of the Bible. Copyright 1989 by the Division of Christian Education of the National Council of the Churches of Christ in the USA. Used by permission.

Library of Congress Cataloging-in-Publication Data

Long, Cynthia L.
    Life after suicide : survival, hope, and healing / Cynthia L. Long. -- 1st ed.
        p. cm.
    ISBN-13: 978-1-7880-2666-9
    ISBN-10: 0-7880-2666-6 (alk. paper)
    1. Suicide. 2. Suicide--Psychological aspects. 3. Bereavement--Psychological aspencts. 4. Suicide--Religious aspects. I. Title.
    HV6545.L75 2011
362.28`3--dc23

For more information about CSS Publishing Company resources, visit our website at www.csspub.com, email us at csr@csspub.com, or call (800) 241-4056.

ISBN-13: 978-0-7880-2666-9
ISBN-10: 0-7880-2666-6

PRINTED IN USA

My Dear Allie,

Where does one begin to describe you and the joy you brought into my life and the lives of others?

You came into my life through a tragedy and then left us in yet another tragic way.

Oh, how I wish things could have turned out differently!

To dwell on the sadness, the hurt, and the regrets won't bring you back. But the pain and the disappointment is so great! You had so much potential. You had so much to offer. You were so gifted! What you gave me in the three years I knew you and loved you is invaluable! I am so grateful for the time we had together. I am different because of you!

Allie, you were like a bird in many ways — tender, fragile, and finicky.

Yet, you were also like a river. You overflowed with laughter, hope, and dreams that ran a mile wide.

You wanted to change the world. Maybe that is why I admired and loved you so. Your heart was so big, and you ignored the obstacles that could block your goals and aspirations.

You wanted to make a difference. You wanted your life to matter! You aspired to counsel and to embrace the weak. You wanted to touch and to love the unlovable. You looked for ways to serve and support the less fortunate.

Your career choices were endless. You considered being a minister, a youth leader, a counselor, a psychologist, and the list went on and on. You could have done anything you set your mind on.

Yet, inside you hurt and you experienced deep emotional pain that most of us couldn't get near. You showed us glances of it once in a while. Then you pushed us away or changed the subject. Your hurt was just too great. Your psychache was too deep to bear any longer.

Oh, Allie. You are free now. You hurt no more.

God has been gracious to you and has answered your prayers.

But those you left behind? We hurt. We grieve. We mourn.

What do I remember the most? I will always remember: the many miles we logged running on the roads, the dinners and dancing with the dogs, hanging out with you in the "UVA room," laughing as you ate lobster for the first time in Corolla, nursing you along when you had your wisdom teeth cut out, and loving you and wishing you were my own daughter.

I will always remember you for the blessing you were in my life. God and your family shared you with me, and I will forever be grateful.

Peace be with you dear one. Know that you were loved. Trust that you will never be forgotten.

Love,
Cynthia

Table of Contents

Chapter 1

Introduction

Cody was the life of the party. He was a 22-year-old man who loved music and spending time with his friends. When a party was taking place, friends could always count on Cody showing up. To his friends, Cody seemed to have it all together. While in high school he was a jock and was very popular. As a young adult he held a job, played in a band, had a girlfriend, and laughed a lot.

After Cody's death, his grandfather told me what Cody's life had been like in the months prior to his suicide. While Cody's life was spiraling downward many of the people around him were unaware of how much emotional pain he was experiencing. Cody developed a drug problem and was required to participate in a substance abuse treatment program. Tired of his moodiness while stoned and his anger when having a bad day at work, Cody's girlfriend had recently broken up with him. No longer could Cody hide his clinical depression. Cody had battled depression for years but failed to admit it to anyone. While several members of his family suspected that the young man was in trouble, Cody played the "tough guy."

While denying that he needed medicine for his depression and adamantly refusing to see a therapist, Cody began to feel hopeless and helpless. Getting motivated for work became a chore. Pretending to be happy around his friends took a lot of energy. Nothing seemed to help his "blues" and down times. Actually they seemed to appear more frequently. Feeling that he had no viable options and wanting his psychological pain to go away, Cody shot himself one Friday night at his family's weekend retreat home. As Cody put the gun inside his mouth, his grandfather and his parents slept soundly in their beds at their respective homes. Never would they have imagined that their life would forever change that Friday night.

This book is written for survivors like Cody's grandfather and his parents. It is written not just for those who have lost a loved one to suicide but it is also for those who want to companion those who are grieving as a result of a suicide. Like cancer, suicide does not just affect one person. Suicide affects those who are living in the aftermath of suicide — family members, friends, neighbors, colleagues, brothers and sisters in Christ from one's church, professional caregivers and even one's pets. Much like how a rock damages a car windshield, the death of a loved one to suicide has a spiraling affect that is hard to put into words.

Friends and family members of people who have died by suicide have a number of ways they can embrace their feelings and thoughts. A survivor of suicide, namely a person who loved or cared about someone who took his or her own life, has several choices of how to live without their loved one. Survivors can address their loss and their feelings "head on" by talking about their feelings and looking for support. Openly discussing their feelings, reading, journaling, and attending grief support groups are several ways that survivors can embrace their feelings. Other survivors choose to keep silent and not openly embrace their feelings and thoughts. This may be due to their own coping skills, due to the depth of their hurt and pain, due to the stigma of suicide, due to what their community or their spiritual beliefs hold about suicide, due to what family members think or expect of them, or a number of other variables.

One of my goals for writing this book is to help suicide survivors who are looking for support and understanding following the death of their loved one. If you are reading this book you are most likely either a suicide survivor who wants to openly embrace and confront your feelings or you are someone who wants to companion others who are survivors. Companioning someone who is grieving entails listening, supporting, and being there for the one who is hurting. As a caring professional who works with the bereaved, as a brother or sister in Christ, as a friend or neighbor, or if you are the one who is grieving, this book will help you learn some basic tenets about how others have lived after the suicide of a loved one.

To protect the privacy of people who have shared their stories with me, names and details of stories have been altered in many cases. Sometimes facts from several stories have been combined or slightly changed in order to respect the confidentiality of people who have shared their stories with me. In several of the cases related in this book, survivors have specifically wanted their stories told in an attempt to help others. One father regularly told his support group, "I don't want Nick to have died in vain." This strong and brave father has worked tirelessly for several years to share his story so that people in his community will never forget Nick but also as a way to reduce the stigma and shame that some people feel following a suicide. Through his openness to tell his story, Dylan is hopeful that someone will benefit from his pain and loss.

As a Grief Support Specialist and a Lutheran minister, I am a better and a more compassionate person because of the many brave and courageous people who have opened their hearts to me and to others by sharing their stories. I am a perpetual student. Many people have taught me a great deal about life after suicide and about resiliency and hope. Throughout this book I hope to honor these survivors by passing along what they have taught me in an attempt to help people like yourself find a way to not only survive, but also to find hope and healing.

Study Group Questions

What was your initial reaction upon reading the comment from Nick's father, "I don't want Nick to have died in vain"?

In the early part of this chapter, the author correlates the effects of death by suicide to "a rock that damages a windshield." How has the suicide in your life "had a spiraling affect" on others?

How many survivors of suicide (defined as "a person who loved or cared about someone who took his or her life") do you know? When thinking about survivors consider relatives, work colleagues, members of your church, acquaintances, and so on.

Chapter 2

The Language

In 1993 I took up the sport of running again. Although I had been a member of the track team in high school, running as an adult was a whole new way of life for me. In high school being a member of the track team was more of a social event than an athletic performance for me. For me simply being part of a team was what was important. Being in one of the "in" cliques and being popular was much more important to me than winning the mile or the two mile race.

When I took up running as a 28-year-old professional, I was entering a whole new arena. I ran for fitness, to be competitive, and to obtain an outlet for work and life stress. One of the things I learned as a young woman was that to enter road races and to be a true runner, I had to learn "the language" of being a runner. Allow me to provide several illustrations here about language.

The tank tops that runners wear are called "singlets." The form one fills out to enter a race is called a "race app," which is short for a "race application." Many road races are not measured in miles, but in kilometers. I quickly learned that 5k races are competitions of 3.1 mile runs. One kilometer equals approximately .62 of one mile.

"Carb loading" means that a runner should eat lots of pasta the day before a race because our bodies need carbohydrates to perform well. The person who runs a race but does not pay the entry fee and therefore does not have a number is called a "bandit." As a non-registered participant in the race, a "bandit" should never cross a finish line. If this is done, race results become completely out of whack!

It did not take me long to learn the difference between a "runner" and a "jogger." Those of us who compete in races, keep track of our mileage, and watch our diets carefully, are usually identified as "runners." "Joggers" are generally folks who do light running for the sake of exercise and tend to be less intense about it than "runners." If you want to offend those of us who compete in road races, call us "joggers" and prepare for a reaction! A comparison might be to call a chef who was trained in a culinary school a "cook." Learning the language of many professions and hobbies is often not only a wise thing to do in terms of social etiquette and fitting in, but it is often an important thing to do in order to better understand one's topic.

The goal of this chapter is to help educate you in the language of suicide. Since this book is about surviving suicide it is important that readers understand some of the language around this topic in order to better understand the content of this book and to also help you obtain a better grasp of this subject matter that has touched your life.

While facilitating a suicide survivor's group I have learned a great deal about suicide. Hearing people's stories and companioning survivors has opened my eyes to a world I did not know in my young adult world. Reading books, attending suicide teleconferences, and experiencing Allison's death by suicide has also opened my eyes to the field now known as "suicidology." This is the field dedicated to the study of suicide that addresses such topics as suicide prevention and suicidal behavior.

One of the greatest suicidologists to date is the late Dr. Edwin Shneidman. Dr. Shneidman was the clinical psychologist who founded the American Association of Suicidology in 1968. Some people have labeled Shneidman "the father of suicide prevention." While he died in 2009, the work of this great man has had a tremendous role and impact on suicidology.

This suicidologist held the belief that the key to preventing suicide is not so much the study of the mental aspects of a person's brain, rather it the study and the understanding of the emotions of individuals. Shneidman was of the opinion that there are two key questions that can help to get at the hurt of suicidal individuals. The questions are: "Where do you hurt?" and "How may I help you?"

As Shneidman grew in his knowledge of this field, he helped to coin new language around this topic that was has been highly stigmatized for years. By stigmatized, I mean that many people feel uncomfortable talking about or addressing this topic for fear of a negative response by others. Unwilling to let stigma keep hurting people from getting help, Shneidman wrote many articles and books over the years in an attempt to break down the barriers of stigma and to educate people about suicide. In 1996 Shneidman's book *The Suicidal Mind* was published. It has become one of the key textbooks today in the field of suicidology. While articulating what he calls "the ten commonalities of suicide," this book is most famous for Shneidman's invention of the term "psychache."

"Psychache" is the deep psychological pain that individuals who attempt suicide often feel. Members of our suicide survivors group often describe their loved ones being in such deep psychological pain that their loved ones did not see any way to end the hurting except by ending their lives. "Psychache" often blinds a person to seeing options or possible ways to resolve their problem or crisis. The psychological pain of a suicidal individual is often so deep that feelings of hopelessness, helplessness, and despair hinder his or her cognitive abilities and fog his or her ability to see any solution except suicide.

"Constriction" is another term used by Shneidman and others that is helpful when attempting to understand folks who have died by suicide. Constriction describes the cognitive state of some suicidal individuals who are of the opinion that the only solution to their problem is to take their life. According to Shneidman's writings, constriction is "the persistent preoccupation with suicide as the solution to their problems" (*Suicide as Psychache*, 1993). A person with constricted thinking might best be described as a person who is experiencing such deep psychological pain that he or she has tunnel vision. Suicide appears to not only be an escape from the pain and the problem but it feels like the only option to the hurting individual.

In his work over the years, Shneidman came to believe that there are ten psychological characteristics that are "common" in over 95% of all deaths from suicides. These are:

> The common purpose of suicide is to seek a solution.
> The common goal of suicide is cessation of consciousness.
> The common stimulus of suicide is unbearable psychological pain.
> The common stressor in suicide is frustrated psychological needs.
> The common emotion in suicide is hopelessness.
> The common cognitive state in suicide is ambivalence.
> The common perceptual state in suicide is constriction.
> The common action in suicide is escape.
> The common interpersonal act in suicide is communication of intention.
> The common pattern in suicide is consistency of lifelong styles.[1]

As Sheidman's work centered around better understanding the person who was suicidal in intention, his work has been paramount in helping suicide survivors. While I mentioned the term "suicide survivor" in the introduction, I want to better clarify its usage here. Some people misunderstand this term and think that a "survivor" is a person who has attempted to kill themselves but was not successful in doing so. That is not the case at all. In the field of suicidology, a "survivor" is a person whose life has been affected by a suicide death. It is also important to note that a "suicide survivor" is not an exclusive term for family members. A best friend, a neighbor, a colleague, a classmate are all people who might consider themselves "survivors" when someone they cared about has died as a result of a death by suicide.

You may have noticed that thus far in this book I have identified people who have died by their own hand as having experienced a "death by suicide." In American culture many people are not sure how to speak of such a death. Do we say that someone "took their own life," "died by their own hand," "killed themselves," or what? It needs to be said here that there is no one way that is right or wrong. However over the years suicidologists and survivors alike have expressed their beliefs that some ways to talk about a suicide death seem better than others.

A personal illustration might best personify this for my readers. Besides my work as a Grief Support Specialist, I have also been an adjunct faculty member at a nearby university. For six years I taught Sociology of Death and Dying at James Madison University in Harrisonburg, Virginia. College students are such great teachers to those of us who hold to the premise that we can learn something new every day! However on one Monday evening four years ago, it was one of my guest speakers who enlightened me with an insight that I have not forgotten. Since that eye-opening evening, I have discovered from reading that many other suicide survivors and suicidologists are in complete agreement with her.

The topic of study for this evening's class was suicide. My guest speaker was the mother of a 24-year-old man who had died by suicide. When I introduced the woman I announced her name and acknowledged how I knew her from the community. Then I said the following, "Ginger's son committed suicide two years ago. Tonight she is going to talk about her son and how his death has affected her life." About fifteen minutes in her lecture, Ginger spoke these words. "When Dr. Long introduced me earlier she said that my son had committed suicide. I don't use that language. I don't find that language useful or helpful to me. I think it is better to say that my son completed suicide or simply that he died by suicide."

This self-assured mother then proceeded to inform the students and me why she did not like the language of "committed suicide." As she spoke I felt like someone had hit me upside the head with a two-by-four. While I felt terrible for offending this woman; at the same time, I was so grateful to have learned new language. Ginger told us to think about how Americans tend to use the verb "commit." Her examples were that we "commit sin, commit crimes, and commit adultery." Generally speaking, when someone commits an act using the English language, it is often negative in connotation.

This sixty-year-old woman then suggested that saying her son "completed suicide" was more acceptable because it did not add the extra negativity and stigma to her son's act. Yes, she was already hurting deeply as a result of her son's death. Why would anyone want to use language when referring to her son that might cause additional hurt and pain? She also helped us to recognize that if in the English language we say that a person "has attempted suicide," would it not make sense then to identify a person who has died by their own hand as "having completed suicide?"

From that day on I have worked hard to use that language in my work with suicide survivors. Many of our group members have also begun to use this language as well. A number of them agree with Ginger that this language is less painful and more helpful to them in coping with their loss.

Another helpful term that will be used in this book is "grief burst." This is a term that describes the feeling that comes over a bereaved person from "out of the blue." Let me offer an example of a "grief burst." Dylan's dad was sitting in his backyard enjoying a drink with his wife as the radio played in the background. The husband and wife were not conversing at the moment but were enjoying the relaxing time together. Dylan's son loved music. The next song that came on the radio was his son's favorite song. Dylan began to weep uncontrollably. Two minutes before, the father was relaxed and was enjoying a peaceful moment at home with his wife. Now he was feeling great sadness as tears filled his eyes. This is a "grief burst."

"Grief bursts" could also be envisioned like this: You are walking along the beach as the sun is coming up. It is peaceful out, and nothing is on your mind but walking. Your mind is on what some of us call "auto pilot." Then all of a sudden a huge wave comes ashore. You are knocked down by its force and find the back of your shorts soaked from the waves. One minute before there was nothing on your mind. Now your world feels completely different. This is a metaphor for what "grief bursts" feel like. One moment you are feeling nothing. Then a song comes on the radio or a person walks by wearing the cologne that your loved one wore. Emotions consume you. Are you going crazy? What is wrong with you? Simply put, you are having a "grief burst." These are normal grief reactions. Bereaved people may have them off and on for years. Give yourself permission to accept them as okay. They are part of the grief experience!

Like any topic or area of interest, the language in and around suicide is always expanding and changing. Words and expressions change over time and are also contextual. Consider doing this when a suicide survivor is using expressions or words that you do not understand: simply listen and wait for the right opportunity to say, "Tell me more about that." "What does that mean to you?" The world of suicidology may be a new world that you have been forced to enter. A man in our suicide survivors group regularly states, "This is a club that I never envisioned joining." If this applies to you, take a breath and allow others to companion you and to support you. Suicide survivors do not need to grieve alone. Let others companion you in your grief journey. And when the time is right, begin to listen to the language that other survivors are using. As you learn a new vocabulary, it is my hope that you will also begin to learn how to cope with this devastating loss in your life.

---

1. Edwin S. Schneidman, *The Suicidal Mind* (Oxford University Press, 1996), p. 131.

Study Guide Questions

How would you describe "psychache" using your own words?

What was your reaction to the use of the expression "completed suicide" as opposed to the well-known expression "committed suicide"? Discuss.

Besides hearing your loved one's favorite song or seeing his or her "look alike," what are examples of other things or experiences that might cause a person to have a "grief burst"?

Chapter 3

Understanding Misconceptions and Risk Factors about Suicide

When someone you love has completed suicide, there are two levels on which you will eventually have to come to acceptance. There is the intellectual acceptance of the suicide death as well as the emotional acceptance. Once receiving the news about a suicide death there often appears to be a huge distance between knowing intellectually that someone has died by suicide and coming to accept that in your heart emotionally. The old saying is something like this, "My head and my heart are miles apart."

In this chapter I will be sharing some of the common misconceptions or myths about suicide. When suicide has become part of your life, it is often helpful to better understand what is factual and what is a myth about people who have completed suicide. I will address the emotional aspects of suicide and articulate upon some of the emotional reactions that suicide survivors feel after someone they love has completed suicide.

As we look back over the last months or years of the life of our loved one, some survivors feel as if we "missed" some of the warning signs. Were there clues that our loved one was hurting so much? Should I have intervened and done something that might have prevented the suicide? Why did he or she not tell me that the pain was just too much to handle?

The truth is that most of us are far from experts on suicidal intentionality. Most people are not familiar with the warning signs of suicidal individuals nor do we know what is myth or fact. In these next pages I will be sharing with you some of the common misconceptions and myths about suicide.

Misconception
People who talk about attempting suicide never do it.
Fact
In a large percentage of completed suicides, the hurting person has given some kind of clue or warning to loved ones.

Misconception
Once a person has made a decision to complete suicide, nothing can stop them from completing the act.
Fact
While there are some people who cannot be stopped from completing suicide, in many cases the person is ambivalent about what they plan to do. Many people who seriously attempt suicide do not really want to die; rather they want their psychological pain to go away.

Misconception
If the person who died did not leave a suicide note then it could not have been a suicide.
Fact
Only one in four or five people leave a suicide note for loved ones to find. The absence of a note does not prove an accidental death or foul play.

Misconception
Once the suicidal crisis is over, the risk for another attempt is over.
Fact
Studies of completed suicides indicate that the highest rates of suicide deaths take place within three months of what appears to be "an improvement" in the person with suicidal

intentions. In other words, just because your loved one seems better right now does not mean that that he or she is no longer at risk. Sometimes the person "seems better" and appears to be more positive or upbeat because he or she has the plan set and is merely waiting for the act to be completed.

Misconception
Conversing about the topic of suicide often gives hurting people the idea to attempt suicide.

Fact
People generally do not get the idea of attempting suicide from another person. Actually the opposite is often more likely. When family members and close friends openly discuss the topic of suicide and the availability of support, hurting people are more inclined to consider the possibility of getting help.

Misconception
Most suicides are completed during the winter or during holiday season.

Fact
Actually most hurting individuals manage to get through the winter and through holidays okay. However once spring arrives and the psychological pain continues, this is when a large number of suicides are completed.

Misconception
Suicide is hereditary.

Fact
While some things like alcoholism and mental health issues can "run in the family," this is not the case with suicide. There is no such thing as a suicide gene. On the other hand, if a person is part of a family where a suicide has already occurred or if a person has witnessed a suicide, this does put

them at a greater risk for suicide than it does for others who have not had those experiences.

Misconception
Completed suicides are more common in certain socio-economic settings than in others.

Fact
Suicide is quite democratic and is generally not found in one socio-economic setting more than another. No economic, social, racial, or age boundaries exempt people from the risk of suicide.

Some Risk Factors for Suicide:
- Person has a history of previous suicide attempts.
- Person has a family member who has died by suicide or violence.
- Person has witnessed another person's suicide.
- Person is suffering from depression or a mental illness.
- Person abuses alcohol or drugs.
- Person has a tendency to act impulsively.
- Person has set very high standards for himself or herself.
- Person has experienced a devastating loss recently such as a traumatic event, a death of someone beloved/highly valued, a career failure, or the breakup of a significant relationship.
- Person has experienced serious or chronic health issues that he or she believes will get much worse.
- Person feels isolated, hopeless, and/or helpless.
- Person has the means of obtaining a lethal weapon.

Be aware that simply because a person has one or two of these risk factors does not mean that the person will attempt suicide. However, when a number of these factors are part of a person's life then a person is more at risk than someone who does not have these risk factors.

Asking Questions

When a car accident happens and a police officer and the police chaplain arrive at the door, most of us know that this is likely an indication that there has been an accident or a death of someone we loved. Upon hearing the news of a death, one of the initial reactions besides shock, denial, and deep sadness is the reaction of asking lots of questions. The people who have gotten the bad news want to know not only the details of what has happened but every little tidbit of information that might help them "put their heads around" what has happened. Months and years later many survivors of suicide are still asking questions with the most frequent one being, "Why?" "Why did he or she complete suicide?"

While friends and family members might tire of hearing the same questions being asked over and over again, many suicidologists and grief counselors are of the opinion that the "search for meaning" into a suicide death is often of benefit to survivors. Certainly survivors are likely to not get many of the answers that they are looking for; however, the struggle with why the death took place is often very beneficial and therapeutic.

As the survivors ask question upon question, their wrestling with the death is a way of helping them to address their pain and to embrace their grief. If on the other hand, a survivor simply buried his grief and did not talk about it or try to make sense of it, this could be a sign that the survivor is repressing his feelings. To put it bluntly, he might be "stuck" in the grief. On the other hand, if a survivor asks questions and struggles to make sense of the death of her loved one to suicide, this is an indication that the survivor is embracing her feelings and is working to try to resolve or to accept what has happened.

One of my colleagues wrote an article where she proposed that perhaps the act of asking the questions is of more therapeutic potential than is finding the answers. The point was that perhaps the power lies in the act of questioning as opposed to getting all the answers. For most suicide survivors the need to ask the same questions over and over again will subside after a significant amount of time has passed. In time many survivors are able to let go of this stage of their grief and will come to be satisfied with partial answers. With time, patience, and the grace of God some suicide survivors will be able to move on in their grief journey and not be preoccupied with the need to wrestle with the "why" question. Their loss has left a hole in their hearts and their loved ones are still missed. The persistent need to make sense of the loss has faded and lessened significantly.

Study Guide Questions

Which of the misconceptions (myths) were you most surprised to learn were not really myths after all? Discuss.

Did any of the risk factors come as a shock/surprise to you?

Has anyone in your discussion group ever known of a suicide survivor who did not struggle with the "why" question? How is the "why" of a death by suicide different from the "why" of other sudden deaths (such as death by a car accident or death by a heart attack)?

Chapter 4

Stories and Emotions of Survivors

Cancer — heart attacks — automobile accidents — strokes — respiratory diseases — many of the people that I have provided grief support to over the years have lost loved ones to the types of deaths that I just listed. While the statistics for the leading causes of death in the United States changes each year, for the last few years heart disease and cancer have been the two leading causes of death for Americans.

Imagine this scenario, if you can. It is in November, a Saturday morning, and you are out buying your weekly groceries. You are pushing your cart down the aisle when you bump into a neighbor who is standing dazed in the frozen foods aisle. Your neighbor Lilly appears sad and withdrawn so you ask, "How have things been going? I haven't seen you in a while." As the tears roll down her cheeks, Lilly says, "Petie died two weeks ago. I still can't believe it." Not knowing what to say next, you say the first thing that enters your mind. "So how did your son die?" Expecting to hear that the twenty-year-old had died in either a hunting accident or from a car wreck, you are shocked to hear what comes out of Lilly's mouth. "Petie took one of his uncle's hunting rifles and shot himself up in the woods."

The thought of death by suicide had not entered your mind as you ask Lilly how her son had died. Now both Lilly and you are speechless. You feel terrible for having asked the question while Petie's mother appears sadder and more lost than she did before you approached her.

In recent years suicide has become one of the leading causes of death in the United States. While national statistics take several years to compile, 2006 figures reveal that suicide was the eleventh leading cause of death for Americans in that year. Likewise, from 2001 to 2005 suicide has ranked the eleventh leading cause of death. In the several years prior to this, suicide has ranked anywhere from the eighth to the eleventh leading cause of death for Americans. In 2006, suicide was ranked the third leading cause of death of young people ages 15 to 24.

In 2006, records indicate that over 33,000 Americans died by suicide, which shows an increase of about 400 suicide deaths from the previous year. While this number seems huge, some professionals in the field of bereavement are of the opinion that this number should actually be higher. This is because medical examiners are sometimes uncertain if some of their reported "accidental deaths" might have truly been suicides. Over the years I have worked with family members that talked about how their loved ones died in single car accidents. However, after hearing some of them describe the accident scene, I have often surmised that the real cause of death might have been suicide. When taking into account the mental state of the person driving the car or the problems in that person's life, suicide may seem the more probable cause of death.

Given the fact that over 33,000 Americans died by suicide in 2006, one has to wonder how many people actually attempted suicide that year but did not die from it. It has been estimated that there are twelve to 25 suicide attempts for every suicide death. Other estimates inform us that there are approximately 750,000 suicide attempts each year in the United States. This is a mind-boggling number and extremely heartbreaking.

Another fact that is hard for many people to fathom is when we break down the number of suicide deaths that take place in the time frame that it takes most of us to sit down and have a quick bite to eat. On average, one suicide takes places every seventeen minutes in the United States. For those of us who regularly watch TV sitcoms, this next number might be hard to imagine. In the one hour that we are entertained by an hour-long TV program, five people in America have died by their own hand. For those of us who eat fast, one person will die in the 15-20 minutes it takes to consume lunch. Statistics also inform us that males complete suicide at a rate that is four times higher than that for females. On the other hand, females attempt suicide three times more often than do males.

What makes males more likely to die from a suicide attempt, you might be wondering? The method of choice is the difference in most cases. The use of firearms is the most common way that men kill themselves. Using a gun is very lethal. When looking at different methods of suicide such as using firearms, hanging, poisoning, suffocating, dying in car accidents, and drowning, males use firearms as their method of choice more often than do females. Currently poisoning is the most lethal method for females who attempt suicide.

Professionals who work with suicide survivors have estimated that for each suicide death that at least six people are intimately and directly affected by the death. My experience working with people who have lost a loved one to suicide is that six is too low a number. It is my opinion that a more accurate number is probably ten people are intimately and directly affected by one suicide. To put this number into perspective, allow me to speculate that if we estimate that 33,000 or more Americans die each year by suicide, then approximately 330,000 lives are intimately touched by those suicides. This is no small figure!

As family members, friends, neighbors, colleagues, and sisters and brothers in Christ live with the effects of a suicide death, there are a myriad of emotions they often experience. Let me state very clearly and succinctly that no two people grieve alike. While people may share similar feelings and have life experiences that parallel in some ways, each person's grief is unique to that person. Like an onion, most people grieve one layer at a time. Grief is a journey. It is not resolved overnight but has to be addressed and experienced one day at a time. Many grief counselors describe grief as being compatible with "work." It takes emotional and physical energy to embrace all the different feelings that are part of a person's grief journey. Grieving takes energy. It is not a passive process; it takes time, energy, and "work." Thus grief is very draining. It can "exhaust" grievers who might describe feeling like they have run a marathon instead of merely having just gotten out of bed.

Experiencing one's grief can be one of life's great challenges. It can be especially difficult if a grieving individual does not understand and recognize that loss changes us. Following the death of a loved one, our lives do become different. We are seldom the same people we were before. People are forever changed by loss.

Many people make the following claim: "I just want life to return to normal. I want things back the way they were before." Those of us who have experienced grief have learned that life never returns to what it was previously. Yes, life can become good again. Grievers can hope to be able to laugh again in the future even though tears and sadness might consume us at the moment. However, grievers also have to learn how to create a "new normal" in our futures. With death comes change. Life will never be exactly as it was before. What was normal before is gone. Learning to live as a suicide survivor means that we have to start a new chapter in life as well as learn how to define what "normal" now might look for us and for our families.

As I have listened to suicide survivors talk about their feelings and their life as a result of a loved one's suicide, I have learned a great deal about the myriad of emotional reactions that survivors feel. I have learned that some people are shocked to learn that other survivors have experienced some of the same emotions that they have felt. Sometimes people feel that they are the only ones who have ever felt this way before. "Am I going crazy?" "What is wrong with me?" "Will this feeling ever go away?" These are all comments I have heard repeatedly from suicide survivors.

There are many emotions a person might feel following a suicide death. In this chapter I will briefly comment on some of the feelings of survivors. However, be mindful that this listing is not all-inclusive nor is it written in a hierarchical order of importance. This chapter will highlight some but not all of the emotions that a survivor might experience following the death of a loved one to suicide.

Shock and Denial

If you are a survivor of suicide, you have most likely already experienced shock. "How could my loved one have been in such pain?" "How could this have happened?" "This isn't real, is it?" When people get that unforgettable phone call or when the police chaplain shows up at your front door, the first feeling that comes over you is often that of shock or denial. You cannot believe what is being communicated to you. You are unable to imagine the emotional pain your loved one must have been in. And it is unfathomable to think that you will never see this person alive again. You feel like you have been hit in the head with a baseball bat. Your ears have taken in the information but your heart feels like it is somewhere else.

As you read earlier, this book is dedicated to the memory of Allison A. Ayers. Allison was a very special person to me. She was my running companion, the daughter I never had, a young lady with the heart the size of a major metropolitan city, and my sister in Christ. I will never forget the evening of November 11, 2008. Briefly home for a few hours before having to return to work to facilitate a grief group, I received a phone call from a newspaper editor that I knew through work. This newspaper editor knew of my relationship with Allison and knew that I would want to know the information that she had just been given. Cassie had heard through an acquaintance that Allison was found dead in her apartment. Even though she was not 100% certain if her source was correct, the newspaper editor wanted me to be aware of the news that was quickly spreading through our community.

In order to check out the accuracy of the news, Cassie encouraged me to contact one of the local pastors in the community who might have more information. The Presbyterian pastor that I was told to call was the pastor of Allison's grandmother. To this day, I am unsure of how this man got the information so much sooner than did some others in our community. It remains a mystery to me.

As I write these words I can remember where I stood as I talked to the newspaper editor and to the Presbyterian pastor on my cell phone. I remember asking the pastor for any and all the information that he had. Was his source reliable? Was Allison really dead? And how had she died? This couldn't be real, could it? I had just spoken to her two nights ago. She seemed to be her normal busy, happy, and hyperactive self. And now she was dead?

After talking to Cassie and to the pastor, I did not know what to do next. I had to leave for work in less than an hour, but I felt like a Mack truck had just run me over. So I did what I always do when bad things happen. I reached out to others for support. I called my best friend and shared with her what I had been told. Together we tried to make sense of what I had just heard. Like me, my best friend could not believe it either. We were numb. We felt frozen. Looking back, I was the perfect example of an individual in shock.

Sadness

Bud is a 73-year-old man in his second marriage. From his first marriage Bud and Ethel had two children, a son and a daughter. Bud's 43-year-old son Jimmy had been battling depression for some time. For about seventeen years Jimmy lived with his girlfriend, Reba. However as the years went on they grew apart, and Jimmy's live-in girlfriend asked him to move out because the relationship was no longer fulfilling for her. This was devastating to Jimmy. Even though he knew that the relationship with his girlfriend was laden with problems, Jimmy hoped that somehow they could work things out. After moving in with his best friend, Jimmy became more depressed and withdrawn. One evening after work Jimmy's former girlfriend came home to find Jimmy lying under a tree dead from a gunshot wound.

Bud and his second wife joined the suicide survivor group not long after Jimmy's death. Sadness continues to be Bud's constant companion. Bud misses talking to Jimmy and doing projects together. But even more than missing the interaction with his son and their mutual love of fixing things together, Bud now realizes that Jimmy must have experienced a huge amount of psychache that would lead him to end his life. When Bud talks about Jimmy's deep psychological pain, Bud's face drops and a deep sorrow fills his heart. Tears often come to Bud's eyes as tries to put words to his feelings. Bud's sadness is shown in his body language and in his facial expressions.

Depression

When someone we love has died it is very common to feel depressed for a while. Once the reality has set in that your loved one has really died, many survivors experience depression. I want to be very honest about this emotional reaction. Learning to live without a family member or a friend who has died from suicide is very difficult! Some survivors have expressed these feelings to me: "Why bother?" "What is there left to live for?" In other words, some survivors feel like their lives are now without purpose. They lack the energy to start tasks. Getting out of bed in the morning can become very difficult. Tears are likely to be a constant companion to suicide survivors at this stage of their grief journey.

Marian and her husband were married for 45 years when he completed suicide. Henry's health had gone downhill for a number of years. This was hard for Henry to accept because he was always a very active and a helpful man in the community. One afternoon Henry asked Marian to walk outside with him when he put a gun to his head as his wife stood in shock, paralyzed by her husband's actions. Marian's depression has been severe since that afternoon twelve months ago. She tells group members that she struggles to get out of bed in the morning. She currently sleeps in the guest room and has not slept in the master bedroom since the day of the suicide.

Marian struggles to live without Henry. They did not interact with many other couples in the last few years of their marriage but spent most of their social time together. Marian wonders what purpose or usefulness her life has without Henry. Tears are her constant companion. While friends periodically call to invite her out, Marian often refuses. Sitting home alone in her house is what occupies most of her waking hours. It is Marian's hope that one day this stage of her grief will pass but for now that seems like an eternity away.

Confusion

Many suicide survivors experience confusion after the death of someone they loved to suicide. Jill is a fifty-year-old middle school teacher whose husband took his life without giving her any clues of his suicidal ideations. She knew that his job was really bothering him and that he battled depression.

However Jill had no idea how much psychological pain her husband must have been in to end his life. She thought their marriage was excellent and that they communicated well together. When her husband completed suicide, Jill wrestled with trying to understand his hurt and his psychache. To this day, she tells friends and family members that she is just as confused about his death as she was the day that it happened. It still makes no sense to her!

In addition to her confusion about why it happened, she also has told me about her confusion in decision making and in her thinking in the weeks and months after his death. Many suicide survivors report that their minds are so overloaded and overwhelmed that making good decisions is almost impossible in the early months following a suicide. Many grief counselors often discourage grievers from making major decisions for one year after a death. In the case of suicide, this is especially good advice. If at all possible, decisions like selling a house, moving away, disposing of previously treasured items, and so on should be postponed for a while until clear thinking is possible.

Blame

When loved ones die it is not uncommon for grievers to blame another person, God, or some factor beyond their control for the death. Not only does this happen when cancer is diagnosed in the latter stages or when a freak accident happens, but blame is a familiar emotional reaction to many suicide survivors. God, the psychiatrist, a former boy-friend or girlfriend, an employer, medication, and so on are sometimes blamed for suicide deaths. When the news is fresh and emotions are raw, sometimes loved ones react to the death by inflicting blame on someone or on something. Accepting the notion that someone could be hurting so much psychologically to end his or her life is a hard pill to swallow for many people! Scapegoating or blaming is often a short-term coping mechanism for many suicide survivors.

Zita's twin sister suffered with mental illness for many years. Even though she was under a doctor's care and was taking her medications, several times Zita's twin communicated her desire to no longer live. Rita was divorced, lived alone, and often withdrew from others when symptoms of her illness were affecting her ability to cope with the challenges of everyday life.

One evening a very depressed Rita told her sister Zita that she really wanted to die. She was so down that she felt like she belonged in the hospital. No stranger to psychiatric units, Rita asked Zita to drive her to the hospital. After an examination the psychiatric staff was of the opinion that Rita was not a serious danger to herself. She was released from the emergency room in a few hours and was sent home with adjustments to her medications. The next day Zita found her sister Rita dead in her garage. She had died by self-inflicted carbon monoxide poisoning.

When I met the grieving sister Zita at her first suicide survivor group meeting, Zita was out for blood. She not only blamed the psychiatric staff at the hospital for her sister's death but was also considering taking legal action against the facility. That night group members allowed Zita to talk through her emotions. After finding the group to be a safe place to share her feelings, a few months later Zita came to realize that suing the hospital would not bring her twin sister back to life. In time group members helped this woman to recognize that her sister's mental illness and her deep depression was the primary cause for her suicide death. A short-term hospital stay might have kept Rita alive that week but most likely her mental instability would have continued to have put her life in risk in the future. In time Zita's need to blame the hospital staff reduced, and she was able to use group time to share other feelings. She also learned that while blaming others is a common grief reaction, it is not a good use of a griever's time or energy.

Anger

Like blame, anger is a very familiar grief reaction to a suicide death. A suicide survivor's anger can be directed at a variety of people. There can be anger at the person who took their life. "Why did you do this to me?" "Don't you realize the pain you would cause to those you left behind?" Anger can be directed at a relative that a survivor blames for the death. If there was a breakup of a relationship, the surviving partner or spouse might hear angry comments directed at him or her. Some survivors are angry at themselves for not seeing the "warning signs" and doing something. Even though intellectually the survivor might know that he or she was not really capable of stopping their loved one from ending his or her life, the survivor's grief and guilt might make them mad at their own powerlessness or lack of ability to control things or people.

One mother I worked with was angry with her son's friends who watched her son pull the trigger on the loaded gun in his hand. Following a night of drinking and horse-playing with a bunch of his buddies, Tasha's son's life came to an end by his own hand. Tasha, to my knowledge, has never expressed anger at her son for having the gun in his hand, rather this mother continues to carry angry feelings toward her son's friends who did nothing to prevent the death.

Leiza, the mother of 22-year-old Cody from the first chapter, became angry when she learned about the death of the young lady in my life named Allison. Leiza told her father that Allison's death was so "selfish." Cody's death was so devastating to her that Leiza could not fathom the pain that Allison's family would be experiencing following Allison's death. It is important to add that Allison's older brother had also died by suicide two years prior to Allison's death. Upon learning about Allison's death, Leiza's initial reaction was that of anger. Venting one's anger at God, the church, the medical staff, or other family members are also other ways displaced anger gets expressed. Because a suicide survivor's pain is so deep and so raw, it does not take much to trigger angry outbursts or displace anger toward the behaviors or the comments of others.

Guilt/Responsibility

When a person dies from cancer, respiratory failure, or a stroke family members are not very likely to feel guilty about their inability to have done something that could have prevented the death. Many causes of death are not a result of something that another person has or has not done. However, when a loved one dies by suicide often family members and friends feel guilty. "Shouldn't I have done something that would have prevented this?" "What if I were a better father, wife, or daughter?"

In hindsight some people think that if they would have just admitted their loved one into a hospital or gotten their beloved to see a psychiatrist that the death might have been prevented. Losing someone to suicide makes many of us feel powerless. Most people do not like feeling that we are powerless or that things are beyond our control. Many of us think that with the right help, any problem can be resolved. However suicide often throws a wrench into our logical thought process.

Death by suicide leads many of us to feel like we might have had some responsibility in the death as a result of our passivity. Several parents who hold the opinion that they should always "be there" for their children have told me they still feel somewhat responsible for their adult children's behaviors because "parents are supposed to be able to fix things for their kids."

Rafael was an ordained minister, a husband, a father, and a brother. One day Rafael was driving his family out to dinner when he lost control of the car and wrecked the family's SUV. That day forever changed the rest of Rafael's life. While his wife was hardly nicked from the wreck, Rafael was paralyzed from the waist down following the collision with a tree and a guardrail. However in addition to his paralysis, the most devastating result from the accident was the death of their daughter. Never a day went by that Rafael did not feel guilt for the accident. If you talked to Rafael he would openly state his belief that the accident was his fault and that he had killed his daughter. Feelings of guilt and self-blame became Rafael's constant companion.

One afternoon Rafael asked his wife to run some errands while he remained at home. Upon her return from the grocery store and the dry cleaner's, Rafael's wife found her husband in the backyard dead from a gunshot wound to his head. Rafael's sister Chica is a regular member of our suicide survivor group. It is Chica's belief that while his paralysis was a hard adjustment to live with following the accident that her big brother could not forgive himself for what he believed was his fault. The younger sister believes that her brother's guilt led to Rafael's death. His suicide note confirms his inner psychological pain and his gnawing feelings of guilt.

Regret

Along the same vein as blame and self-anger, some survivors carry a deep sense of regret following a suicide death. In hindsight some survivors feel that they should have told their loved one more often that they loved them or should have spent more time with that special person. Saying hurtful things when in a bad mood or leaving things unsaid are often actions that survivors may carry for a long time unless in time they come to realize that these thoughts are stopping them from being able to move toward healing. Some survivors may need to seek professional help in order to work toward forgiving themselves for feelings they hold inside like regret, self-blame, or unresolved issues they had with their loved one.

Embarrassment and Shame

Because many people in our communities are uncomfortable talking about suicide and as a result of the stigma of suicide in American culture, many survivors often acknowledge feeling embarrassed when a loved one has died by suicide. Some survivors have spoken about feeling self-conscious that friends and family members are judging them or talking about them behind their backs. This is very painful.

Shame is another emotion that often goes hand in hand with embarrassment. Usually shame is related to guilt, embarrassment, or feeling that somehow their relationship with their loved one was inadequate or not healthy.

In a support group I facilitated for grievers who had lost loved ones to a variety of deaths like cancer, car accidents, heart attacks, and old age, a thirty-year-old sister came to the group to express her grief over her brother's death. Izzy told group members that her brother had survived being in Iraq for three years, then died in a single car accident. As the weeks went by in the support group we learned that Izzy's brother most likely suffered from PTSD (Post Traumatic Stress Disorder) and depression; however, his sister was convinced that his death was purely accidental. While no one will ever probably know the true cause of death since the accident scene did not prove the cause of the accident with 100% clarity, I came to believe that this man might have died by suicide. However, his sister would never allow herself to consider that as a possible cause for his death.

When someone in the group alluded that perhaps her brother's death might not have been an accident, Izzy was adamant his death was a freaky and unexplained accident. She could not grasp the notion that her war-hero brother might have not been able to cope with his PTSD and his depression and opted out of life by creating a car accident. I truly believe that if the police report verified that his death was by suicide, Izzy would have experienced deep-seeded embarrassment. She wanted to keep the picture of her brother in her mind as "war-hero" not "suicide completer." Even the hint of such a thing in the group seemed to throw this woman for a loop. "Not my brother!"

Feeling Alone

When I was a young woman I had heard the expression, "You can be at a party and still feel alone," but I did not truly understand what that meant until I had more life experience under my belt. As an extravert and a person who "wears my feelings on my sleeve," it took me years of companioning grieving people before I understood that being in the midst of a crowd of people has little to do with feeling connected or understood. Some people can be sitting in a room with a dozen or more people, but still feel empty and lonely inside.

Suicide survivors often can relate to this phenomenon. Grieving can be a very lonely experience. Even when a survivor opens up to others and shares his or her inner thoughts and feelings, the survivor may not feel heard or understood. Because not all of the people we interact with have the best listening skills, lots of grievers learn in time to keep their feelings to themselves. When people change the subject, act uncomfortable around us, or try to offer a quick "fix" or solution to our problem, this lends itself to grievers clamming up.

Even though a suicide survivor might be out socializing in the community or might be seen in town talking to friends at a ball game or at church, this does not necessarily equate to this person feeling listened to or supported. Many survivors have told me that grieving is a very lonely journey. At times I have felt this emotion myself. A number of months after Allison's suicide, many of my friends and family members stopped bringing up Allison's name around me. Did they think that I would forget her in six months or stop missing her? Did they think that since I wasn't a blood relative that my feeling like her "second mom" would dissolve after her death? Grieving after Allison's death did feel lonely to me.

Preoccupation

When the suicide has just happened and the survivor is feeling "raw" with pain, a sense of preoccupation with the death is quite normal. Death by suicide is not something you can just file away in your brain and agree to pull it out later and deal with it. When a loved one dies unexpectedly by suicide, a survivor should expect to struggle with the loss. Unlike cancer or other kinds of terminal illness where death is expected, death by suicide rocks most people's worlds. Constantly thinking about the death and your loved one is a more likely grief reaction than is being able to "put your emotions on hold" for a while. Many suicide survivors experience feelings of preoccupation with the death for quite some time. It is often the only thing that survivors can think about for a long time.

Dylan told me that when Nick died by hanging that he felt like there was a fog shadowing his every thought and action. It took a long time for Dylan to be able to have thoughts about topics other than Nick for many months. Survivors also talk about feeling guilty when the time comes that they are able to think about something else for a brief period of time. It is almost as if preoccupation with the death has become the norm, and then when other things like a joyful thought or a moment of laughter takes place that the survivor feels guilt or surprise by this change in emotion. Preoccupation is a very familiar emotion to new survivors.

Inability to Concentrate

Similar in some ways to preoccupation is the grief reaction where survivors cannot concentrate at work or on projects at home. The death is so painful and so disturbing that the survivor cannot think of anything else even when he or she is trying very hard to accomplish tasks or get work done. Audrey's 65-year-old mother took her own life. This came as a complete shock to Audrey and her father. While Audrey's mother had a number of serious health problems that were not improving, no one in the family had any idea of the depth of this woman's inner pain. After her mother's death Audrey reported that she was unable to be productive at work. Her inability to be herself at home was even noticed by Audrey's children who did not know the true cause of their grandmother's death. All the children knew was that their mother was not herself since their grandmother's death and that their mother was often somewhere else in her thoughts and would leave many of her tasks undone at home.

Relief

While the majority of suicide survivors would seldom admit it out loud, in some cases death by suicide is actually a relief. When the loved one has suffered from a mental health disorder for years or when clinical depression has paralyzed a loved one's ability to enjoy life or function effectively, the death of this person might come as a relief to loved ones. In cases where a loved one has felt tormented by his or her quality of life or when a person has held the opinion that life was awful with no chance of improvement, the death of this

41

person though heartbreaking might come with some feelings of relief and peace.

Suzanna's twenty-year-old son battled mental health issues for years. While medicated and getting counseling, Bernard knew that his life would never be like that of his cousins and his friends. When Suzanna and her husband discovered Bernard's dead body, they were greatly saddened; yet relieved at the same time. No longer would they watch their son's illness destroy his soul. They would miss Bernard forever, but Suzanna felt comfort in her Christian belief that Bernard was now healed. The promise of resurrected life kept Suzanna going while others around her struggled to make sense of what had happened. Suzanna told a number of us at a support group that she was very comfortable identifying some feelings of relief following Bernard's death.

Tabitha also felt a great sense of relief when her son-in-law killed himself. As a faithful Christian woman, she felt deeply sorry for the pain that was in his heart but at the same time, she was relieved that when he killed himself he did not shoot her daughter before putting the gun inside his own mouth. Tabitha's son-in-law had lost his children in a custody battle with his first wife and was struggling with this along with his bi-polar illness. After stopping his medication one day he kidnapped his current wife from whom he was temporarily estranged. Gun in hand he threatened to kill her before he went on to take his own life. When the police came to Tabitha's home to state that her kidnapped daughter was safe but her son-in-law was dead, Tabitha felt a tremendous sense of relief.

Hopelessness/Helplessness

When someone we love takes his or her own life, we feel like we might have been able to prevent this somehow and some of us feel helpless and out of control. Most human beings like to think that we can control the most important things in our lives. Many of us like to think that we have control over what we eat, where we live, and where we work. And some of us even try to control our loved ones even though we know that this is not really possible!

A death by suicide makes some survivors feel like we have failed. How is it that we can influence some people and their decisions but when it comes to matters of life and death, we are truly powerless over people's choices? Try as hard as we might, we cannot stop someone from ending his or her own life. Feelings of helplessness and not having control over things that are truly meaningful to us leave some survivors feeling hopeless as well. "If we cannot protect those we love what does that say about ourselves?" "Is life really worthwhile when the ones we love the most are beyond our reach?"

In the early stages of their grief, some suicide survivors feel that there is little hope left in their world. The death of their loved one has left them feeling that life does not have much meaning right now. Some survivors talk about a huge void or emptiness in their bodies.

Suicidal Thoughts

It is not uncommon for some suicide survivors to feel like they would like to join their loved one in death. Even though the survivor would not want to endure suffering or pain to experience the reunion, the idea of a reunion in heaven or in the afterlife is appealing to some survivors. The good news is that this emotional reaction frequently passes in time. Most survivors do not act on their suicidal thoughts. One of the hardest parts of this grief stage is for the friends and family members of survivors to hear the suicidal ideations put into words. This can be downright frightening to folks who have already lost one loved one to suicide. One man whose wife died by suicide, talked to me several times about his suicidal thoughts. While he had no plans in his head to end his life, I believe that his talking about his wanting to die was one of the only ways he knew how to talk about his sadness. In his case, I suspect that some of his talk was attention seeking. I saw no warning signs of a real suicidal crisis in his life. I suspect that his psychiatrist would agree with me since this bereaved husband has not been recently hospitalized but is being monitored and counseled regularly by his psychiatrist. In this case, both husband and wife have suffered with lifetime issues of mental health and abuse. However the surviving spouse is more resilient than he wants to admit.

Loss of Interest in Socializing

As is the case with other types of death, sometimes family members and close friends choose to withdraw for a while and will distance themselves from friends and relatives. Some people need "their space" for a while and decline dinner invitations and will not answer the telephone or respond to email messages. In many cases, this behavior should not alarm those who are close to the survivor. In many cases, this stage will pass and will lessen with time. Some bereaved individuals need "alone time," and socializing is just too difficult for them at the present time. As friends and family we need to respect and honor this if this is the case with your special person.

Loss of Trust

Intimacy issues can be affected by grief. Some suicide survivors question their ability to trust others or perhaps themselves when a suicide death comes as a complete shock to them. "Am I no longer able to be a good judge of what is going on around me?" "Am I naïve in that I can't tell when my closest friends are experiencing a major life crisis?" When a survivor feels so raw with feelings of hurt and loss, he or she might even push his or her closest loved ones away.

One survivor of suicide told the college students in my Death and Dying Class that he and his wife were not intimate for two years following the suicide death of his adult child. He explained that he was just feeling so raw and hurt inside that he could not allow himself to be close to anyone. He could not open himself up to anyone, not even his wife at this difficult time in his life. I held the belief that this was his way of trying to build a cocoon around himself. It was as if he was attempting to put a big shield around his body and his heart.

Acceptance

I believe that most grief counselors and suicidologists would say that their hope for their clients is that one day the suicide survivor will eventually come to acceptance of the suicide deaths in their lives. Over the years, professionals in the field of bereavement have used a variety of terms to express this stage in the grief journey of the bereaved. Terms such as "accepting" the loss, "resolving" the loss, "adapting" to the loss, and so on have all been used to articulate the hope that one day the hurting person will be able to gradually accept the death and move toward a new chapter in his or her life without his or her loved one.

Remember, suicide survivors will never forget their loved ones. However one can hope that in time the hole in their hearts will become smaller, and new relationships and new interests can be pursued as survivors decide they are capable of and desire to make meaningful futures. Accepting the death does not mean forgetting the people who have died. Rather it means that survivors have come to realize that they need to move forward with life and start a new chapter without their loved ones.

Study Guide Questions

What are other words that might describe the grief reaction of "denial" or "shock"? Can you recall times in your life when you felt "frozen" upon hearing tragic news?

Anger is a very common grief reaction. Identify ways that people can vent or express their anger in ways that are healthy and not harmful to themselves or to others. Also discuss why you think some people are reluctant to admit feelings of anger. Is this merely an individual choice, or does it have cultural significance?

Why are some people reluctant to own feelings of relief when death happens to a loved one? Does this have cultural significance? Is it more acceptable to acknowledge one's relief over the death of a loved one in other cultures where the views of death and afterlife are different from that of Americans?

Chapter 5

What You Can Do
to Survive and to Cope

Parents are often very familiar with the routine of teenagers begging them to "just let me sleep in for a little longer" before getting up and getting dressed in the morning. In some cases of school-aged children and adolescents resisting getting out of bed is a result of their not wanting to go to school. For others this is merely an action of a child's being tired or just plain lazy. As many parents will attest, lots of children and teenagers are hard to arouse in the morning!

Some grieving individuals also struggle with getting out of bed in the morning. However, their reasons for getting out of bed are often very different from those of children and adolescents. Difficulty getting out of bed is sometimes the result of depression, of not wanting to live without his or her loved one, or it is a way of avoiding one's feelings of loss and pain. A first step in learning how to survive the death of a loved one to suicide is a very basic one. This step is called "getting out of bed in the morning." Even when you do not know how you will cope with the new day, the first thing a suicide survivor needs to do daily is to get up and get moving. When asked, "What did you do in the first few months following your loved one's suicide?" survivors told me with very serious looks on their faces, "I got out of bed." Getting up and getting dressed is one of the basic steps of coping with the death of a loved one.

In this chapter I will address some of the things that suicide survivors do to live with the death of their loved one. While every griever copes in his or her own unique way, I have learned that there are some coping techniques that seem to be fairly common with suicide survivors. Let's review some of the things that grievers do in an attempt to live following the suicide death of someone loved. Even though many of us have felt powerless following the death of someone we loved to suicide, many of us are learning while we were powerless over the action of our loved one we are not powerless over our own actions or behaviors. We do have control over how we grieve and respond to the death of people that we love!

While we might not have control over things like grief bursts or what others say to us, we do have the ability to choose how we are going to live in the upcoming days, months, and years following our loss. We can give up on life and the future or we can embrace our feelings and work toward creating a new life — one without our loved one in it. As we know our futures will be different now than we had anticipated and hoped prior to the death, we can "work through" the loss and embrace our survival without our special person in it.

Getting out of bed and getting dressed is one of the first things a suicide survivor has to do on the day after learning about the death. This is often easier said than done. Over the years I have learned that when some grieving people cannot eat or sleep they often visit their primary care physician for help. Because physicians are not trained as grief counselors and because their time with patients is often a matter of minutes and seconds, not hours, some physicians choose to prescribe anti-depressants or sleeping medications for their newly bereaved patients. In some cases this might not be a bad thing; in other cases this can lead to problems.

Taking anti-depressants too soon after a loss can numb a person's feelings so that they are buried or repressed. Even though this might seem like a great way to avoid one's pain, this can really hinder the normal grieving process. It is normal to feel raw, shock, hopeless, devastated, and powerless in the first days and weeks following a suicide. If one's medications numb these feelings, what will happen when the anti-depressants are stopped? Guess what? These feelings have not disappeared; rather, they have somehow gotten temporarily buried. Grief reactions from a death are likely to resurface if they have been buried and are not addressed. When this takes place your friends and family members may have moved beyond their initial feelings of shock, raw pain, and devastation, and you are now just beginning your grief journey. This is not a good place to be.

Another concern with grievers taking anti-depressants to numb or dull their pain is that grievers can become so accustomed to their sleep aids or anti-depressants that they do not want to stop using them. Because physicians only see their patients when they come to the office and are not seeing them daily like neighbors and family members, it is hard for physicians to know when to stop writing refills for prescriptions.

Please do not hear the message that anti-depressants and sleep medications are bad. That is not true. In some cases, using medications for a short-term basis when grieving may be beneficial and appropriate. However prescription medications are not the end all and be all! Never should medications be a substitute for doing the "grief work." Grievers need to experience their pain and loss and not repress it. Some medications can help grievers who are working through their grief. Medications should never be used to bury or to inhibit one's grief so that it can be avoided!

Along this same vein, it needs to be mentioned that excessive use of alcohol or prescription drugs is not a good idea either. While "self-medicating" might help a person feel better temporarily, alcohol is actually a depressant that will often leave the survivor feeling worse. Likewise taking anti-anxiety medications, pain killers, and the like, to an excess could make a survivor's situation much worse than before taking these "numbing" medications.

For a number of years scientists have been studying the chemical makeup of tears. Some researchers have come to believe that tears from emotional upset like sadness or grief have a different chemical makeup than regular tears that lubricate and clean the eyes. These researchers are of the opinion that tears resulting from the release of strong emotions like sadness and grief remove toxins from the body and also release endorphins, which help to alleviate pain. In other words, crying when experiencing grief not only helps us feel better but it also helps our body to move toward healing.

One of the things that many survivors of suicide find helpful in coping with their pain and loss is to allow themselves permission to cry. While crying will not bring our loves ones back, it does help some grievers to express pain and to find temporary relief from the bottled-up emotions. American culture in recent years has discouraged boys and men from crying by communicating that tears are a sign of weakness. I would like to acknowledge that in my work with grieving people, I have found tears do have therapeutic value for both male and female grievers. If you feel sad and want to cry, do not worry about what others around you might say to you or comment behind your back. Your grief is yours! You have the right to express your feelings in a variety of ways, one of which is shedding tears. I am reminded that when Jesus learned that his friend Lazarus had died that we are told, "Jesus began to weep" (John 11:35 NRSV). If our Lord can cry, why can't we?

One of the healthiest things a suicide survivor can do to cope with the death of a loved one is to be open and honest with your friends, colleagues, neighbors, family members, and your sisters and brothers in Christ. Because the people around you are not "mind readers," you need to honestly and openly communicate to them what you are feeling and what you do and do not want or need in terms of support. It is very important you tell the folks around you what they can do to be helpful to you in your grief journey. Whether you need a listening ear, a walking companion, a helper with errands, a partner to attend a support group with you, or if you feel you just need some space for while, this is best communicated out loud instead of assuming that your closest friends and family members know what you need by telepathy. As the saying goes, "Honesty is the best policy."

Suicide survivors frequently ask about how to talk to the children and grandchildren in their lives about the cause of death of their loved one. Maggie is a sixty-year-old woman whose husband battled depression for many years. While her adult children knew that Dad had some struggles with feelings of melancholy over the years, the notion of suicide as the cause of his sudden death never entered into their minds. For many months following her husband's suicide Maggie did not tell her children or grandchildren how her husband of thirty years had died. Then one day a cousin leaked the news to one of Maggie's grown daughters. On the telephone the next morning Maggie's daughter vented her anger toward her mother for not being honest with her about how her father died. To this day, tension still exists between Maggie and her three children because Maggie chose to not tell her children the truth initially.

My experience is people need to be honest with their family members about the suicide. While very small children might be the exception to the rule here, in most cases being honest about the nature of the death is generally the best. I have learned over the years that even knowing that a suicide has taken place is very painful to hear, it is usually more painful to discover the truth months and years down the road through a friend or a distant relative.

Everyone grieves in their own way and along their own timeline. Currently I know a woman who has not told her teenage children how their beloved grandmother died.

Audrey believes the truth would destroy the positive image her children have of their grandmother. Even though group members have tried to encourage Audrey to tell her children the truth before more time passes, we also recognize that this is Audrey's journey and not ours. We have voiced our opinions but trust that Audrey will follow her heart and her head and know what is best.

I facilitate a suicide survivor group that meets twice a month. Many in our community have found this to be a safe place to share their pain and to receive support and companionship in their grief journeys. We do not have to grieve alone! Others are willing to companion us in our journeys if we are willing to open ourselves up to such an opportunity. There are many suicide support groups throughout the United States. At the back of this book in the last chapter there is a list of resources on how to go about finding a support group in your area. If you are a new suicide survivor or if you have never fully embraced your loss, I would encourage you to consider attending a support group. In the final chapter of the book I have also listed the website for the American Foundation for Suicide Prevention, which sponsors an annual suicide teleconference that is shown in various cities throughout the United States each November. Survivors find that watching the teleconference and participating in the dialogue following the presentation to be very beneficial.

Support groups are a place where you are able to openly talk about all of your feelings without being judged or labeled. These groups are also places where you can share stories and memories openly. In the "grief world" some of us identify the sharing of memories and the telling of stories about our loved ones as "continuing bonds." Keeping the memories of loved ones alive is very important to many of us who are suicide survivors. Most of us will always want to know someone is available to listen to us when we want to recall a special story or talk about a special memory about our loved one. In this way we can keep memories of our loved ones alive while simultaneously moving forward with our lives. There is an anonymous quote that I find very helpful that highlights this sentiment: "Life must be lived forward, but understood backward." Attending a support group and making friends is a helpful way for many survivors to recall our pasts, but also work toward creating a new future without our loved one.

Some survivors of suicide find reading books about suicide can be helpful to them as they progress in their grief journeys. While in the initial stage of their loss some survivors are not ready yet to understand more about the mind of someone who is suicidal, in time many survivors find "bibliotherapy" helpful. There are many books on the market addressing the mind and the some of the thought patterns of people who have been suicidal in the past. This can help survivors better understand the psychache and the emotional pain their loved one might have experienced. Also, there are books about how to live and survive after a completed suicide of a loved one. Books like these can equip us with tools and tips for grieving well and surviving our loss.

Since each survivor's grief is different, each person's coping techniques will be different as well. However, there do seem to be several coping techniques that help most grievers. Getting proper rest, exercising on a regular basis, journaling, and giving oneself permission to laugh once in a while are a few of the techniques that I have personally found helpful when grieving. Many of the grievers that I have companioned over the years would echo that sentiment wholeheartedly. Perhaps the best way to survive the death of a loved one to suicide is to listen to your own heart and your own body. Take time to listen to the still small voice in the silent moments of your life. Try not to stay so busy that you do not have time to work through and to embrace your grief. Experiment with different coping techniques to find some that work for you. Or talk to a friend in your suicide survivor group or your counselor if you are having difficulty getting through the day. Remember no one has to grieve alone!

Study Guide Questions

Why do you think getting out of bed and getting dressed is a hard task for many suicide survivors?

Do you think attending grief support groups is beneficial to group participants? Discuss the pros and cons of grief groups.

In this chapter the author provides a number of ways an individual can survive and cope following a loved one's death by suicide. In Danielle Steel's *His Bright Light: The Story of Nick Traina* and in Judy Collins's *Sanity and Grace: A Journey of Suicide, Survival, and Strength* these two women write about what they did to survive and cope following the loss of their sons. Can you think of other books that are similar in style and content?

Chapter 6

How Others Can Be of Support to Suicide Survivors

For those of us who are part of the baptized body of Christ, we tend to look at being part of the community a little differently than others who are not part of the Christian community. In the waters of Holy Baptism God adopts us and makes us part of the body of Christ and the people of God. In baptism believers are promised the forgiveness of our sins and the gift of eternal salvation. As water is poured over the head of a newly baptized person, this individual becomes part of the body of Christ and is united in the death and resurrection of Jesus Christ.

Once a person is baptized we are changed. We are never the same again. We are marked with the cross of Christ and are part of the universal priesthood of all believers. In other words, we are part of a community of faith. Being a Christian essentially means being part of "community." We are no longer lone rangers!

As baptized children of God, God calls us through our baptisms to love and to support one another. While some people talk about their faith as a personal and a private matter, often Christians understand that Christianity is a communal religion. We live, worship, celebrate, and suffer together.

In his letter to the Christians in Corinth the apostle Paul writes about how Christians are part of the body of Christ: "Indeed, the body does not consist of one member but of many. If the foot would say, 'Because I am not a hand, I do not belong to the body,' that would not make it any less a part of the body. If the ear would say, 'Because I am not an eye, I do not belong to the body,' that would not make it any less a part of the body. As it is, there are many members, yet one body" (1 Corinthians 12:14-16, 20 NRSV).

Paul goes on to write about how believers share in the lives of other believers: "If one member suffers, all suffer together with it; if one member is honored, all rejoice together with us" (1 Corinthians 12:26 NRSV). In other words, if a Christian is grieving the death of a loved one then his or her brothers or sisters in Christ are likewise sharing his or her pain and sadness. As we live in community, we also grieve in community!

Conrad is a man in his mid-sixties whose wife shot herself in the basement of their home. While his wife had some health issues that were significant, Conrad had no idea of the depth of his wife's emotional pain. Tanya's death came as a complete shock to Conrad. As he talks about their marriage and his wife's mental condition prior to the suicide, Conrad is adamant about the fact that he had been given no clues or warnings of her intent to kill herself. One summer day when Conrad went inside his home after being outside for a few hours doing yard work, he could not believe his eyes. The woman who was outside working with him two hours earlier was now lying dead in a pool of blood. She died from a self-inflicted gunshot wound to the head.

Anyone who has ever been around Conrad for more than fifteen or twenty minutes would describe this man as very outgoing and as a person with a huge heart. Other folks might tell you that this man is one who "doesn't know a stranger." With his down-home smile, Conrad is very approachable and down to earth. As a result of his outgoing and kind nature, Conrad has many friends and a huge social network. When his wife died, Conrad's friends, neighbors, coworkers, his church family, and his family members reached out to him and provided him with a great deal of support. Now some two years after Tanya's death, many of these same people continue to love and support Conrad in many ways.

When suicide becomes part of a person's world, many survivors would say we feel like the foundation under us has been rocked. We no longer look at things we way we used to. What was once "normal" no longer exists for us. Our equilibrium has disappeared and fog and pain surround us. Without the support and love of others and without the grace of God, many suicide survivors would fall apart and slip into hopeless despair. The role of friends, neighbors, colleagues, family members, and sisters and brothers in Christ is crucial! Without others in our lives survival following a suicide death might feel impossible. However, when others are there for us listening to us, hugging us, praying for us, and serving in Jesus Christ's stead, some of us have discovered our pain is more bearable.

In the days and months following Tanya's death, Conrad's friends and family members have "been there" for this bereaved man. Conrad has told me over and over how many phone calls and dinner invitations he has received and continues to receive. When I am with Conrad his cell phone is constantly ringing. While Conrad misses his wife greatly and is still trying to figure out how to live without her, simultaneously, he is not without companionship. Those around him have loved him and companioned him throughout his grief journey. Conrad does not lack for friends or for support. I believe that he would tell you that without people in his life and without God he would not still be alive. His grief might have led him down the same road as his wife. When suicidal thoughts have entered his mind, his faith and his relationships have kept him alive.

Likewise, when Nicolai died by suicide his wife Hannah was very fortunate to have great support from her friends and her colleagues at work. Hannah works for a lawyer in a small town legal practice. Several weeks after her husband completed suicide I got a phone call from her boss asking if I would be willing to come to his office and sit down with Hannah and his staff to talk about how they could support Hannah following Nicolai's death. Because her boss is a very caring and compassionate man and because his Christian faith has taught him the value of uplifting and supporting those who are hurting, Hannah is blessed. She has a wonderful work environment. When she was numb and frozen in the initial stages of her grief journey, she received understanding and support from her colleagues at work and was given permission to take whatever time off or whatever space she needed. This is an invaluable gift!

Growing up in a small town in Virginia I was taught well about "Southern hospitality" and about Christian support in times of crisis and loss. As a child I was on the giving and the receiving end of meals delivered following the death of loved ones. I can also remember the plethora of phone calls and cards that our family received when my grandfather died and when my brothers suffered head injuries from an automobile and a bike accident. While the giver does not always realize the value of their chicken casserole or their sympathy card with the handwritten note inside, many grievers will tell you of the enormous value and love they felt from these acts of kindness.

When a Christian congregation or a friend remembers you in prayer, this is a gift of great benefit. As the saying goes, "The power of prayer changes lives!" Remember suicide survivors often feel alone in their loss. Realizing that others are holding us in prayer is a gift beyond measure!

People ask me when I am giving presentations on grief and loss issues, "What can I do to help someone who is grieving?" To this I reply that one of the best things that you can do to help someone coping with a suicide death is to "be there." "Being there" means that you are physically and emotionally present for your friend or loved one. As you are there for this person it would be helpful to engage in what is called "active listening." This entails listening to the person who is hurting and doing only a limited amount of talking. When you are "actively listening" it is helpful to paraphrase or summarize back what you have heard the other person say. This helps the person who is sharing to know you have "heard" what has been said. Most grieving people do not want advice from you nor do they expect you to take their pain away. What they often need is someone to listen to them.

Sometimes we call this process a "compassionate presence" or a "ministry of presence." This is the role that a person plays in someone else's life where your primary job is to show your caring presence and your compassion and concern for the individual. When you are there for someone with no ulterior motive and you are willing to "companion them" by listening and supporting them, you are often received very openly and appreciatively.

Sometimes suicide survivors feel like they are being judged by others. Because people sometimes want to blame someone for a completed suicide, family members or close friends sometimes feel like others might think they are somehow to blame for their loved one's death. One of the greatest gifts you can give to someone in this position is to provide support in a loving and non-judgmental way. This is when the notes, brief phone calls, and the casseroles or dinner invitations are a way to show your support. You are showing support through ways where words are not necessary and sometimes not even welcome.

Sometimes when a death or a crisis happens in our lives, we learn who it is that we can count on. I have heard this expression used many times by attendees of my support groups over the years. Sometimes the people that we thought would companion us for months and years to come are no where to be found while other people in our lives shock us by their faithful friendship and ongoing support. When someone is there for us in a helpful way that we did not expect this is like winning the lottery. It is a blessing that we have never expected. On the other hand, when someone we love or were close to us disappoints us by their absence or by speaking words that are harmful, we sometimes feel that we have been struck with another loss. People can disappoint us. People can let us down. And people can say things that are well meaning but chill us to the bone.

One of the best tips I can offer to folks who are grieving as a result of a death by suicide is to suggest they ask folks for what they need. Survivors need to tell their friends, family members, neighbors, colleagues, and brothers and sisters in Christ what they need in terms of support and what they do not want or need. People are not mind readers even though they might think they know you pretty well. Survivors, please tell people what you need when they ask you, "What can I do to help?" Be honest with them. If you do not know what might help you that is fine; however, if you know of some things that would make you feel uncomfortable or would offend you then speak the truth with love.

Christians are called to share the sufferings and the joys of others. This is hard to do when we do not know if or how others might want us to companion them. Similar to a good marriage, communication is a key to a meaningful relationship. Respect someone if they ask you to give them space or some time. You can still remember them in prayer. And when someone specifically asks for something, try your best to do it if you are able and if it is an appropriate request.

Dorcas's husband battled depression for at least half of the years of their marriage. Once an outgoing and lively man, for the last twenty years of their married life Duncan did not want to socialize any more and spent hours in his study at home reading and napping. When Duncan shot himself, Dorcas' church family wanted to provide her with lots of emotional support. However Dorcas wanted to grieve privately and not mourn publicly. A mutual friend of ours asked me to call Dorcas to check in on her and to invite her to our suicide survivors group. I made a phone call to Dorcas and invited her for a cup of coffee.

During our hour-long conversation Dorcas was very up front with me, telling me she was a private person and did not want to share her grief with folks at church or in the community. While she told me she did have several close friends, she made it very clear she wanted me and others to respect her privacy. She wanted to grieve in her own way and by her own methods. I did what Dorcas asked and have never brought it up again. When I see her at church functions in our community I always hug her and let her know that I care about her, but I respect her wish and do not ask her things like: "How are you doing? How is your grief going?"

One of the couples who attend our suicide survivor group got the exact opposite response when they asked for privacy and some "alone time" to process their son's death. Nancy's oldest son died by suicide, leaving Nancy and her husband reeling in shock and disbelief. Nancy and Van had no idea their 41-year-old son was hurting so deeply emotionally. Some two years later, Nancy still wrestles with understanding why her son completed suicide. Since the death took place in December the upcoming holiday was something that Nancy and Van were dreading. They asked their out of town relatives to not visit and to respect their need for privacy. They were not ready to talk about the death and needed some time to absorb their new reality.

Van's sister was planning a visit to other relatives around Christmas and called Van to say she wanted to visit with him and Nancy. Van made it clear his wife was not up to any visits noting she had been very clear. She was not ready to talk to anyone right now about her son. During the Christmas holiday a knock came at Van and Nancy's home one afternoon. It was Van's sister. Because she had lost her husband to a drowning twenty years earlier she thought she could tell Nancy how to handle her grief. She showed up unwanted and unwelcome at her brother and sister-in-law's doorstep several days after Christmas. This story was relayed to me in writing by Nancy when she learned that I was writing this book. She asked me to please include it here in hope that other people might learn from her experience. She titled her two-page story, "Well-meaning Visitor Is an Intruder." Need I add more to make the point?

Two other requests from suicide survivors stand out as I write this chapter. Lydia is a seventy-year-old woman who had two sons. Her youngest son lived out of state with his wife and three children. Each year Lydia would make two trips to visit with her son and his family. Playing with her grandchildren and giving them gifts meant a lot to Lydia. When her son died by suicide, Lydia told the participants in our support group one night that she not only felt like she lost her son when he put the gun to his head but she also felt like she lost her grandchildren as well. Since her son's death a year and a half ago, Lydia has only seen her grandchildren once.

When Lydia calls her daughter-in-law's home in hopes of talking to her grandchildren, only occasionally is anyone home. Phone calls are seldom returned. When she mentions possibly visiting, her daughter-in-law claims that it does not suit their schedule. Lydia's request is a simple one. She wants to see her grandchildren and continue a relationship with them. While losing her son is traumatic enough, Lydia fears she might actually lose three other members of her family. At this point of her grief journey, it seems as though her request is falling upon deaf ears. It is my hope and prayer that one day things will change, and this grieving woman will be allowed to continue a relationship with her three grandchildren. Time will tell if her request is heard and honored.

Genny is a young widow with three small children. When her son completed suicide, she had three children at home under the age of ten. Because of the age of her children and her work schedule it was difficult for Genny to attend support group meetings. One of the things that Genny requested from neighbors and friends was some respite time away from her children. While she loved them and wanted to be with them, at times she needed some to be alone and also some time to be with adults. We saw Genny for about three or four meetings and then never saw her again.

I do not know if her neighbors and friends did not realize that Genny was honestly asking for what she needed at the time and never got it, or whether or not she ever made her request known to more than one or two people. The sad part of Genny's story is that when I spoke to her a year later she still seemed overwhelmed by being a single parent and was still talking about needing a break once in a while. Again, I remind people to listen and honor what is being asked of you when you say, "If there is anything that I can do just let me know." If you are speaking those words in an attempt to say something, please offer a hug and a smile instead.

One of the things friends and loved ones realize when they arrive at the home of a family who have lost a loved one to death is that each person in the family will grieve differently. While this has already been shared in this book, this next point has not yet been made. Males and females grieve differently. Some of these differences are based on individual differences. One of the main reasons that men and women grieve differently is due to sex-role conditioning. In North American culture the norm has been for male children to be taught to not express sadness and to be strong while female children are usually allowed to cry and express their sadness. There are always exceptions to this rule but in more homes in the United States than not, little boys are told to be strong and are discouraged from crying while little girls are given more freedom in expressing their emotions and feelings.

When children become adults they do not forget what they were taught at home and in their communities. My experience as a grief support specialist confirms what I have read over the years about gender difference with grieving people. Men tend to be less comfortable with showing their emotions in public while women feel less inhibited from doing so. Also women seem more comfortable attending grief support groups while their male counterparts are sometimes more reluctant to come to a meeting alone. When you are trying to be supportive to friends or loved ones who are grieving, do not expect a husband and a wife to grieve the same way for a child who has completed suicide. Or if you have an adult brother and an adult sister who have lost a parent to suicide do not think that the way you support and companion one will be the same way that works for the other sibling.

Remembering anniversaries and special days are well received by someone who has lost a loved one to death. The anniversary of the suicide, one's birthday, Christmas, Easter, Mother's Day/Father's Day, Valentine's Day, and so on can be very difficult days for suicide survivors. Inviting someone out to lunch or for a cup of coffee may be one way to help someone who is hurting to realize that they are not forgotten. If the person who died was a child, Mother's Day or Father's Day may be a very difficult day. If the death involved a spouse then Valentine's Day or a wedding anniversary may be a hard time for a survivor. Cards, a telephone call, or a brief visit are other ways to remind suicide survivors that they are not forgotten.

Another thing survivors tell me over the years has helped them to embrace their grief and to remember their loved one is the use of rituals and special ceremonies. While most families will hold some kind of funeral, memorial service, interment or celebration of life, this is not always the case. In some instances the person who died specifically asked to have no ceremony or funeral to mark his or her death. Sometimes the family member in charge of arrangements and decision-making is not deeply religious or spiritual and chooses not to have a memorial service or funeral. That is most certainly the choice and prerogative of each family.

However, for most of the families I have worked with over the years the funeral, memorial service, interment, or celebration of life was very helpful in gathering people together to share stories, to obtain emotional support, and to hear words of comfort and support by a religious leader or by someone in the community that the family respects and admires. In most cases, some type of ceremony helps the family to accept the loss and begin the grief process. When the family is Christian, the service usually involves a combination of some remembrances about the person who died as well as the proclamation that Jesus Christ died and rose from the grave to open the way to eternal life for his followers. Christian funerals are most often a time when mourners publicly share their pain and sorrow and also find comfort and celebration in the promise of resurrected life.

Sometimes in the months and years after the death, family members will choose to do some kind of additional ritual or ceremony to remember their loved one who has died. This might take the form in things like a tree dedication in a park, a brick dedication in a public garden, a bench being placed in front of a school or at a golf course, or a plaque being placed in a hospital, grief center, or the like.

Scholarships are sometimes established in memory of someone who has died so that the person who died is never forgotten. College buildings have been built in memory of loved ones as have football stadiums. There are many options of how to memorialize a loved one and remember them. As no two people grieve alike, no two families will memorialize alike. Spend some time with your friends and family members discussing what might be an appropriate choice given your resources, your beliefs, and your loved one's interests and beliefs. The possibilities are endless! Again, I encourage you to remember we do not live alone, and we do not grieve alone. We live, love, and grieve in community!

Study Guide Questions

If suicide were to touch someone in your "social circle," would you prefer it to be someone like Conrad or someone like Dorcas? Why?

What was your reaction to Nancy and Van's story of the unwanted visitor that Nancy called "the Intruder"?

Spend some time in the group brainstorming ways that people can be supportive to suicide survivors. What are some specific things that can be done to show care, support, and love?

Chapter 7

Faith, the Church, and Suicide

Over the years as I have worked with suicide survivors, one of the struggles that surfaces with a number of survivors is that of their relationship with God. Suicide can shake the foundation of one's core beliefs. While a person is very active in his or her Christian congregation as a result of a deep faith in Jesus Christ, sometimes an unexplained death like suicide can lead this individual to question some of his or her previous beliefs and assumptions about God and God's involvement in our lives. On the other hand, I've witnessed the fact that the death of a loved one can bring other people closer to God and simultaneously strengthen their faith and trust in God.

As everyone grieves in their own unique way, so too do people express their faith and live out their spirituality in their own way. Even though a group of people might belong to the same Christian congregation and be part of a large national denomination, it does not mean that these people are robots professing identical beliefs and values. How a person lives out his or her life as a Christian believer and what core beliefs he or she holds is most likely as different as cola is from lemonade. Both cola and lemonade are drinks, but each has its own set of unique attributes and flavor.

There is no way to completely cover all of the different positions and views that Christians have held about suicide since the church came into existence in the first century. That could be a book in and of itself! In this chapter I will review key positions held by two leaders in the early church, look at references to suicide in the Bible, and also look at the current teachings held by the Catholic church and the

67

Evangelical Lutheran Church in America. In addition to this I will articulate how I believe that God views the person who has died by suicide and how God feels about those of us who are survivors. Do be aware that this part of the chapter is subjective and is written from my theological perspective and through the lens of my life experience.

In the very early church one of the primary theologians that shaped early Christian thought was Saint Augustine of Hippo. Augustine was a fifth-century bishop and doctor of the early church and is best known for his work *The City of God*. Some Christians have lauded Augustine as one of the most important figures in the development of Western Christianity. In his writing *The City of God* Augustine outright condemned the act of suicide. Having said this, I think it is important to note the context of Augustine's thought. During this time period many of the suicides that were completed were enacted by women who had been raped and held the opinion that they were no longer pure or by women who thought dying by suicide was better than being forced to have sex against their wills. In Augustine's thinking and context, it appears as though death by suicide was more a concern relating to morality and religious virtue than it was a concern that was related to mental health disorders, depression, or the deep emotional pain of some individuals.

The other well-known leader and theologian of the Catholic church who condemned suicides was Saint Thomas Aquinas. Aquinas was a scholar and theologian who lived in the thirteenth century. In *Summa Theologica*, Aquinas wrote that dying by suicide is a sin against three parties: oneself, one's neighbor, and God. Both Augustine and Aquinas believed that completing suicide was a form of murder and thus it constituted committing a mortal sin. In their view, when a person died by suicide, there was no time for repentance.

If we shift gears for a moment and look at several Protestant theologians we would find a more grace-filled response to suicide. Both Dietrich Bonhoeffer, the German Lutheran pastor who participated in the German Resistance Movement against Nazism, and Karl Barth, Swiss Reformed theologian, considered by some as one of the most important theologians of the twentieth century, held positions that were more grace-filled and forgiveness-oriented than either Augustine or Aquinas's positions. Bonhoefffer and Barth expressed their beliefs that even though taking of one's life is sinful by its very nature; at the same time, they reiterated their positions that the grace and forgiveness of God would be extended to those who had completed suicide. In their eyes, God's forgiveness would extend to all sins including suicide.

When suicide survivors are Christians they are interested in discovering how the biblical writers addressed the topic of suicide over the years. While no biblical book states a specific theological position on suicide per se, there are seven completed suicides reported in the Old and New Testaments. In the Bible we also encounter a number of people from the Old and New Testaments who experienced great despair but never succumbed to suicide. For example, while Moses, Elijah, and Jonah wanted God to end their misery, their eventual deaths were not the result of their earlier despair or emotional distress.

Six of the seven accounts where suicides are referred to in the Bible are found in the Old Testament while only one reference comes from the New Testament. I will briefly summarize the six suicides found in the Old Testament beginning with Samson's story. These stories are not being shared here in the chronological order of when they are believed to have taken place, rather the order I am following is to recount them as they are found in the Old Testament.

The first suicide in the Old Testament is found in the book referred to as Judges. The suicide reported here is that of Abimelech, the son of Gideon. Most people who have studied Jewish and Christian history refer to Abimelech as a wicked man. Abimelech proclaimed himself king of Shechem after the death of his father Gideon. However, before Abimelech took over the throne he first killed his half brothers (seventy in number) in order to assure his position of obtaining the throne.

Not long after Abimelech took power, a large number of people in Shechem revolted against the king and his followers. Because of the uprising and unhappiness surrounding his leadership Abimelech moved to Thebez. The biblical writer reports that one day a rebellion broke out in Shechem, and fighting took place at the Tower of Shechem. While Abimelech was trying to burn down the tower, a woman took advantage of the opportunity before her and threw a large millstone at Abimelech. The large stone hit his head and broke his skull. Because of his arrogance and pride and not wanting the stigma that a woman had brought about his death, Abimelech ordered his armor-bearer (someone over whom he had authority) to kill him. By enacting this assisted suicide plot, the king attempted to save his image and avoid the shame of dying at the hands of a woman (Judges 9).

Samson, one of the judges of the southern tribe of Israel called Dan, is well known in Jewish and Christian history for his superhuman strength and for his extremely long hair. Born to a previously barren couple, his parents were told to never allow their son to cut his hair. His parents were also informed that Samson would help to deliver Israel from the hand of their enemy the Philistines.

One day after falling in love with Delilah, the Philistines abducted Samson and gouged out his eyes and cut his hair. Later after his hair grew back and his strength returned, Samson created a plan to enact revenge upon the Philistines.

In Judges 16 we are told that Samson called to God and announced that he wanted to die with the Philistines. In his act of revenge against them he used his superhuman strength to pull down the pillars of a large house filled with Philistines, and he died along with them. Current language might call this act "murder-suicide" while in Samson's lifetime his action would have been understood by his contemporaries and being done with the intent of killing his enemies. The bottom line is that Samson took his own life in an act of final vengeance.

Another suicide that is found in the Old Testament is that of Saul and then that of his armor-bearer. Saul was the first king of the united kingdom of Israel. Anointed by the prophet Samuel, Saul reigned from Gibeah. His tenure lasted from 1047 to 1007. While on the battlefield one day against the Philistines, the biblical writer reports that three of Saul's sons were killed and Saul was severely wounded. Knowing his army was being defeated at Gilboa, he was badly injured, and he might be tortured if captured by his enemies, Saul ordered his armor-bearer to kill him. Unable to do what was asked of him, the armor-bearer did not consent. He could not kill his king and his commander. Unable to convince his companion to end his life, Saul fell on his own sword and died in front of his armor-bearer. In response to this, the biblical writer reports the armor-bearer followed suit and also died by his own sword (1 Samuel 31, 1 Chronicles 10).

Another of the suicides found in the Old Testament recalls the death of Ahithophel in the book of 2 Samuel. Ahithophel was a man of great wisdom and was considered a sage of his time. Initially he was a counselor to David, the second king of Israel. Later Ahithophel parted ways with David and shifted his loyalty to David's son Absalom who rebelled against his father and his father's power.

Initially Absalom took the advice of Ahithopel and followed his counsel. Following Absalom's revolt and

71

uprising against his father, Absalom was crowned in Hebron and Ahithophel was pleased to be on the same team with Absalom.

One day as Absalom was preparing his troops for a huge battle with David and his troops, Absalom allowed Hushai, a spy of his father David, to influence a key political decision regarding battle strategy. Hushai's advice was taken over against that of Ahithopel. As one might imagine, this caused great turmoil for Ahithopel. Not long after learning that Absalom had listened to Hushai and not to him, the biblical writer tells us that the wise counselor went to his home, set his affairs in order, and then hanged himself. Biblical scholars are not clear as to the exact reason for Ahithopel's suicide. Was it purely because his counsel was not taken and he was angry or possibly embarrassed by this? Or, did he complete suicide because he thought that David might exact retribution against him one day? No one will ever know why Absalom planned his suicide and completed it (2 Samuel 17).

Zimri's suicide is the final suicide and is found in the Old Testament book 1 Kings. Outside of this account in 1 Kings little has been reported about Zimri. According to the author of 1 Kings, Zimri was a military commander who murdered King Elah at Tizrah. Following Elah's death, Zimri succeeded him as king for seven days. Members of the army did not approve of Zimri's kingship and rise to power so they elected Omri as king. As one can see illustrated in several of the above mentioned Old Testament stories, when problems arose politically, fighting and warfare often broke out. One day when Omri and his army besieged Tizrah, Zimri reacted by setting fire to the royal palace at Tizrah. As the flames and the fire overtook the royal palace, Zimri remained inside where he died. Similar to Samson's death, Zimri's plan to destroy the royal house was an act of revenge as well as an act of suicide (1 Kings 16).

From the New Testament there is only one suicide reported. This is the death of one of Jesus' twelve apostles, Judas of Iscariot. After Judas betrayed his Lord by turning Jesus over to the Jewish authorities, we learn from the gospel of Matthew that Judas hanged himself. Very little is reported about Judas' suicide. We are told that Judas took the money he was paid to identify Jesus, confessed his error in betraying Jesus, and threw down a handful of coins inside the temple. After doing this, the biblical writer tells us that Judas left the temple and hanged himself.

While this account is found in Matthew 27:5, a different accounting of how Judas died is reported in Acts. From that account found in Acts 1:16-20 we are informed that Judas died as a result of a fall. We know little about the fall except that Judas fell "headlong" and that his bowels "gushed out" as part of his body "burst open." Since there are conflicting stories about the nature of Judas' death, we cannot claim with any certainty that Judas' death was that of suicide.

In addition to the seven biblical examples of suicide that I have commented upon here, I also want to highlight the details of a mass suicide that is well-known throughout Jewish and Christian history. According to Josephus, the well-known first century Jewish Roman historian, about 960 died in a mass suicide on the mountain fortress called Masada in 73 AD. The background for the mass suicide is this: In 70 AD the Romans destroyed the city of Jerusalem as well as the Jew's holy temple. Due to the Romans power, a splinter group of Jewish believers referred to by some as "zealots" fled Jerusalem and retreated to the mountain fortress called Masada. Masada was built by Herod the Great between 37 to 31 BC and was thought to be built as his safe house in the event of an emergency.

After the destruction of the second temple in 70 AD, this group of Jewish zealots sought to find a place to live and hide from the Romans. Around 73 AD the Roman army attacked the fortress at Masada in an attempt to get the Jewish zealots out of their hiding place. The attempt to break in was not easy as the mountaintop fortress was extremely secure. Finally as the Roman army was getting close to breaking through an opening in the stone wall through the use of a large battering ram, the leaders of the Jewish group decided that it would be better to die their own way than to be taken prisoners by their enemies.

Josephus reports that the head of each household was responsible for killing all the members of each household. Then the men drew lots to determine who was to kill the other men. After all the men had killed each other, the last man completed suicide. While about 960 people died in this act of mass suicide, two women and five children survived because they hid in a cistern. The choice between suicide or capture must have been a very difficult decision for these religious zealots. One has to wonder what the zealots thought would have happened to them if they had been captured by the Romans. One can only imagine that rapes, beatings, torture, and then eventual deaths must have been imagined in order for suicide to have been the best option.

I now want to change direction to highlight how several Christian denominations today view those who have died by suicide. While some more conservative Christian denominations consider suicide self-murder and therefore a grave sin against God, other Christian denominations lean more toward the grace side than the judgment side. Even though many people in our communities have heard some of their Christian neighbors state that salvation is not possible when a death has taken place as a result of suicide, others of us do not perceive suicide as unforgivable sin. Because of God's grace and Christ's death on the cross for us, some of us cling to God's promise of grace and forgiveness, which gives us hope and comfort. Several Christian denominations today are spending more time in their social statements addressing the great suffering and psychological pain that suicidal people often experience while also encouraging believers to trust in God's love and mercy as opposed to focusing in on the seriousness of the sin as some denominations do.

While many people today are of the opinion that the Catholic church condemns suicide as unpardonable, in actuality the current catechism of the Catholic church is more grace-oriented than some people know.

From the Second Edition of The Catechism of the Catholic Church, revised in accordance with the official Latin text promulgated by Pope John Paul II in 1997, we find this section under Article 5 — The Fifth Commandment:

Suicide

2280 Everyone is responsible for his life before God who has given it to him. It is God who remains the sovereign Master of life. We are obliged to accept life gratefully and preserve it for his honor and the salvation of our souls. We are stewards, not owners, of the life God has entrusted to us. It is not ours to dispose of.

2281 Suicide contradicts the natural inclination of the human being to preserve and perpetuate his life. It is gravely contrary to the just love of self. It likewise offends love of neighbor because it unjustly breaks the ties of solidarity with family, nation, and other human societies to which we continue to have obligations. Suicide is contrary to love for the living God.

2282 If suicide is committed with the intention of setting an example, especially to the young, it also takes on the gravity of scandal. Voluntary co-operation in suicide is contrary to the moral law.

Grave psychological disturbances, anguish, or grave fear of hardship, suffering, or torture can diminish the responsibility of the one committing suicide.

2283 We should not despair of the eternal salvation of persons who have taken their own lives. By ways known to him alone, God can provide the opportunity for salutary repentance. The Church prays for persons who have taken their own lives.

The Evangelical Lutheran Church in America, the denomination under which I am ordained, has a "Social Message on Suicide Prevention" written in 1999 and then copyrighted in 2003. This statement on suicide recognizes that there are some people who despair life and live feeling hopeless and tormented. The message lists suicide statistics, risk factors, attitudes surrounding suicide, and the role of the church to receive and to offer help. The section of the social message that I find most helpful is the section under "Receiving and Giving Help" where the writers of the document uplift the invaluable role of congregation members and pastors for suicide survivors. Like the Catholic Church's Catechism, the Lutheran position encourages people to trust God's love and mercy in regards to matters of hope and resurrected life.

Under the section "Receiving and Giving Hope," I want to quote the fifth and final paragraph of that section:

> "When a suicide does occur, congregations and pastors minister to the bereaved and deceased through Christian burial and their loving support. Funerals are not occasions either to condemn or idealize an act of suicide, but times to proclaim that suicide and death itself do not place one beyond the communion of saints. Because of Christ's death and resurrection for us, we entrust a troubled person to God's love and mercy with the promise that "whether we live or whether we die, we are the Lord's" (Romans 14:7). Pastor and congregation need to offer intentional and sensitive care for the family and loved ones of the deceased for

76

some time and offer them the opportunity to become part of a support group for survivors" (p. 8).

As a pastor of God's church and as a person who has lost a loved one to suicide, I firmly believe God looks at those people who have died by suicide with loving and understanding eyes. I believe God understands brokenness, woundedness, and psychache better than any human being could ever grasp. If Martin Luther viewed the church as "the inn and the infirmary for those who are sick and are in need of being made well" (Lecture on Romans, *Luther's Works*, Vol. 25), one has to wonder how much deeper and greater is God's understanding and love for those who are deeply ill emotionally and psychologically. I cannot imagine anything but a God who opens his arms up to a dying person and welcomes this hurting and suffering child into the safe haven of resurrected life. I envision a God who conveys this welcoming message to the person who has died by suicide: "Your pain is now over. My son died and rose from the dead for you. Peace is your gift for eternity. Welcome home, dear one."

Along a similar vein, I envision God reaching out to those of us who are suicide survivors and reminding us the cross is that which we can cling to. The promise of resurrected life made in baptism gives survivors comfort, strength, and hope for tomorrow. We do not grieve alone. I trust God is reminding us at the very moment of our deepest pain that he is right there with us, crying with us, questioning what might have been different, and bleeding alongside with us. God not only shares our suffering and our hurt, but God has overcome death and the power of hell and has won the victory through Jesus' death and resurrection. Death and defeat will not have the last word; rather, the cross and the empty tomb prevail.

During the days, months, and years when survivors cry out to God wondering where God is or how this could have happened to their loved ones, this is the very time that God reaches down to us and feeds us with his word of hope and life and when the holy sacraments (Baptism and Communion) are administered as God's food and sustenance for his people. When survivors cry out, "Where are you God?" it is to the empty tomb where God is to be found. Trusting that God sacrificed his only Son Jesus for us and for our salvation, Christians can find comfort knowing that we are united in our grief and also in our hope of resurrected life. While survivors might sometimes feel alone and abandoned by God; God promises to always be with us. God never abandons his children! God's heart is a heart of compassion, and God's embrace is one of continual strength, comfort, and steadfast presence.

Christians find that verses of scripture can be a source of great comfort when they are grieving and are feeling down. There are dozens and dozens of verses that could be shared here, but for the sake of brevity I am only going to share six.

> O Lord my God, I cried to you for help, and you have healed me. O Lord, you brought up my soul from Sheol, restored me to life from among those gone down to the Pit. Sing praises to the Lord, O you his faithful ones, and give thanks to his holy name. For his anger is but for a moment; his favor is for a lifetime. Weeping may linger for the night, but joy comes with the morning.
> — Psalm 30:2-5

> I lift up my eyes to the hills — from where is my help to come? My help comes from the Lord, who made heaven and earth. He will not let your foot be moved; he who keeps you will not slumber. He who keeps Israel will neither slumber nor sleep. The Lord is your keeper; the Lord is your shade at your right hand. The sun shall not strike you by day, nor the moon by night. The Lord will keep you from all evil; he will keep

your life. The Lord will keep your going out and your coming in from this time on and forevermore.

— Psalm 121:1-8

Do not let your hearts be troubled. Believe in God, believe also in me. In my Father's house there are many dwelling places. If it were not so, would I have told you that I go to prepare a place for you? And if I go and prepare a place for you, I will come again and will take you to myself, so that where I am, there you may be also. And you know the way to the place where I am going. Thomas said to him, "Lord, we do not know where you are going. How can we know the way?" Jesus said to him, "I am the way, and the truth and the life. No one comes to the Father except through me.

— John 14:1-6

What then are we to say about these things? If God is for us, who is against us? He who did not withhold his own Son, but everything else? Who will bring any charge against God's elect? It is God who justified. Who is to condemn? It is Christ Jesus, who died, yes, who was raised, who is at the right hand of God, who indeed intercedes for us. Who will separate us from the love of Christ? Will hardship, or distress, or persecution, or famine, or nakedness, or peril, or sword? No, in all these things we are more than conquerors through him who loved us. For I am convinced that neither death, nor life, nor angels, nor rulers, nor things present, nor things to come, nor powers, nor heights, nor depth, nor anything in all creation, will be able to separate us from the love of God in Christ Jesus our Lord.

— Romans 8:31-35, 37-39

My grace is sufficient for you, for power is made perfect in weakness.

— 2 Corinthians 12:9a

I can do all things through him who strengthens me.

— Philippians 4:13

While nothing can be done to reverse the suicide and bring a person back to earthly life, many Christians are comforted by the promise of resurrected life as well as the promise that nothing can separate us from the love of God. While some Christians have doubted God's presence when bad things have happened in their lives, other Christians have discovered it in the hard times in life that God's grace and his sacraments have sustained us and kept us going. I believe that a great many people of faith would agree with me in saying that being part of the Christian community is a wonderful gift from God. While we not only share a common faith rooted in the promise of new life in Jesus Christ, many of us as Christian believers also find amazing support and consolation from the Bible and from our brothers and sisters in Christ.

Study Guide Questions

Discuss the scriptures that close this chapter. After reviewing each one separately, try to come up with "the overarching message" conveyed in these verses? How do these passages collectively portray God?

Psalm 30:2-5
Psalm 121:1-8
John 14:1-6
Romans 8:31-35, 37-39
2 Corinthians 12:9a
Philippians 4:13

What influence does one's culture and one's life experience have on an individual's perception of completed suicide? Are these influences greater than or on an equal plane with one's spiritual beliefs and values?

Chapter 8

Survival, Hope, and Healing

A few days after I had finishing writing the seventh chapter of this book I got a call from one of my closest friends. Through her tears and sobs Bree eventually was able to get out what she had wanted to tell me. She had just learned that her brother Jeff had shot himself to death, and that she was in the car heading out to support her one surviving parent. During his 46 years of life Jeff had undergone over a dozen surgeries in addition to battling depression and experiencing a broken marriage. Even though Jeff's death did not come as a surprise to either Bree or me, Bree told me something very insightful right after her brother's memorial service had ended. "I know that I'm going to need you in the weeks and months ahead. I know that I've got a long road ahead of me."

Bree's comments tell you that my girlfriend recognizes her life will never be the same since Jeff's death. In our many conversations before Jeff's suicide, Bree and I had talked about how we might cope if either of us ever lost a family member to suicide. While we both knew that a death by suicide could happen in our families, neither of us was really prepared for Jeff's death. However Bree quickly discovered she was soon to enter unchartered territory — a life without her dear brother Jeff and a future of "what if's" and "why's."

Bree is now a survivor of suicide. While her brother's actions were his own choice, becoming a member of this group was not of Bree's choosing. Because Bree is a resilient and a strong woman with a great support system and a strong faith, I trust she will learn how to survive and how to live without her "baby" brother. However, Bree's journey will last for months and years. There is no quick fix or easy remedy for how she will cope and survive. She will take a couple steps forward and then will fall back once in a while. But she will survive! The unknown question is what will she do to survive this loss and by what steps will she eventually experience healing and wholeness again?

Bree's grief journey will be hers and hers alone. She will learn by trial and error, along with lots of tears and hugs along the way. It will not be an easy journey, but it is a necessary journey. Like all of us who are survivors know, our journeys are lived "one day at a time."

This final chapter of my book offers a few tips to survivors about how to begin to create your new life after the suicide of someone you loved. This chapter will offer ideas and suggestions on how you might go about living as a suicide survivor. No one can prescribe an "end all and be all" of how to cope and live after a completed suicide, but I want to offer a few words of wisdom here. Take what works for you or feels right, and ignore what does not seem plausible for you. Notice that I am not telling you to "get over" the death or "just forget about it" as some folks are inclined to tell survivors.

A person who has lost a loved one to death does not "get over" his or her grief like he or she gets over the flu. There is no cure for grief because grief is not a disease. Grief is a normal response to a loss. Grief is how we respond when someone or something we care about has been taken or removed from us. Learning to live without a loved one or someone special is a process, a journey. One has to embrace his pain and his emotions in order to move toward healing and more hopeful days ahead. A grieving person will soon learn that life will never go back to the way it was before the death. Death changes us. We are never the same as we were before.

People who are in the initial stages of grief often cry out that they want things to get back to normal — to the way things used to be. Those of us who have experienced loss before know that things never go back to the way they used to be. Instead, we have to create a "new normal." Bree and other suicide survivors soon realize that we must start a new chapter in our lives now. And this chapter of life is a chapter without the person who has died. While we will always miss the person who has died, in time we can hope to remember our loved one without all the accompanying hurt and pain that we felt in the early stages of our grief journey.

When a suicide first happens most survivors talk about a huge hole in their hearts. The pain is so raw and new. The hole feels like it is almost as large as one's whole chest. In time, many survivors discover the hole seems to get a little smaller. Then as months and years pass a tiny hole remains, but the feelings of rawness and hopelessness have gone. With the support of caring people in your life and by the grace of God, survivors can learn to live and function with this tiny hole in our hearts. Many survivors report that in time the pain does lessen as the memories begin to bring joy and comfort instead of pain and heartache.

Forgiveness is often a part of a survivor's grief journey. Some survivors have to learn to forgive the person who completed suicide. If a survivor can better understand the role psychache might have played in her loved one's life, then she may be able to think of the act of completing suicide as a means of ending one's emotional pain instead of focusing in on all the "what if's" and "why's." Sometimes a survivor will have to forgive himself for the death. While no one is responsible for anyone's actions other than one's own, some people think that they can affect or control the actions of others. The sooner we realize that we are not responsible for anyone but ourselves, the more freely we are able to live. If you are still blaming yourself for what you might have done, could have done differently, or for what you might have missed, stop for a moment and ask God to help you forgive yourself. If God can forgive us, should we not forgive ourselves as well?

As an athlete and as a professional, I can be very demanding and hard on myself. When I compete in sporting events like a road race or a golf tournament, I want to do really well. When invited to give a lecture or a workshop I expect my presentation to be a good one. Sometimes I can be my own worst enemy and my biggest critic. However when it comes to grief, we need to remember to give ourselves a break and to let others support us like we might support them. Some of us are inclined to set high standards for ourselves and to expect quick and gratifying results. This does not work with grief!

Just as there is no right or wrong way to grieve, there is no set way to grieve. It is as individual an experience as is a person's handwriting. What I suggest here is to be patient with yourself. Allow yourself to grieve as your body and your heart guides you. Do not expect your grief patterns to be the same pattern you use for work or for your hobbies. For example, if you are an "overachiever" at work, do not expect that behavior to carry over into the grief arena. You cannot set a goal to feel better in a certain number of weeks or months and expect that to happen.

If you are a person who is generally strong and well put together, do not expect yourself to hold it together well in the initial months following a suicide death of a loved one. The old rules do not apply here. My best advice is to give yourself a break and do not create a list of how you should and should not be doing in the next few months and years. Allow your grief journey to develop and flow. If possible, do not micromanage your emotions.

Open yourself up to new people and new relationships in your lives. Sometimes new friendships can develop following a tragic experience. There is an old saying that "when one door shuts, another door opens." I am not saying that we replace people with others. We do not replace people like we replace cars, appliances, or worn out running shoes. Rather I am saying that sometimes we grow and we form new relationships after a loss has taken place. Over the years I have heard countless stories of survivors who reported that after a significant amount of time had passed, they realized that a few good things had come out of their tragedy. While no one would ever desire to go through a loss or a tragic event in order to discover something good down the road, it appears as if sometimes God brings hope and new opportunities out of chaos.

In the early chapters of this book I wrote about the father named Dylan who lost his 22-year-old son to suicide. Several times over the past five years Dylan shared an insight in our suicide survivor group that is so profound that I want to share it in this final chapter.

While in the early stages of one's grief suicide survivors like Dylan are often consumed by the method of his or her loved one's death. In time Dylan was able to recall and to cherish the memories and the great moments together. While the thoughts of the suicide might fog and pervade a survivor's initial thoughts, Dylan shared that after a significant amount of time had passed he discovered the method of his son's death would not define or mark Nick's life. Dylan has told group members numerous times that he will not allow suicide to define his son's life. Yes, Nick did die by his own hand, but the previous years of his life is how Dylan is choosing to remember his beloved son.

The final bit of advice I offer to suicide survivors is to encourage you to keep the memories of your loved ones alive. While I may sound like a broken record in repeating this piece of information, it is too important to not mention at the end of this book. The concept of "continuing bonds" is crucial to surviving the death of a loved one. It is very healing and therapeutic to continue to tell the stories about our loved ones and to keep their memories in our hearts and on our tongues. Never allow the stigma of suicide or the discomfort of others hinder you from remembering your special person. Allison may have died two and a half years ago but as long as we remember her and talk about her she is alive. She will never be forgotten as long as her loved ones and friends remember her. This is a key ingredient to survival, healing, and hope!

As a Christian resource I want to close this book by quoting part of a psalm from the Old Testament book, Lamentations. The several verses that I quote are part of a lament from an individual who is feeling distressed and is in need of some hope and assurance from God. This person's witness is a reminder to believers that God hears our cries and gives us hope. Whether we are grieving a death or are seeking vindication like the psalmist, God never abandons his children.

> I called on your name, O Lord, from the depths of the pit; you heard my plea, "Do not close your ear to my cry for help, but give me relief!" You came near when I called on you; you said, "Do not fear!" You have taken up my cause, O Lord, you have redeemed my life.

May the grace of God and the presence of loved ones and friends in your life support you and companion you as you embrace your pain and move toward survival, hope, and healing.

Study Guide Questions

What was your initial reaction to the author's statement, "A person who has lost a loved one to death does not 'get over' his or her grief like he or she gets over the flu"? How

86

prevalent is this "getting over one's grief" language in current society?

How can you help others who are grieving a loss to practice the "continuing bonds" concept? As a child were you taught to talk about and to remember loved ones who died, or was talking about the dead discouraged?

Can people "survive" and perhaps even thrive after a loved one has died by suicide? Compare the resiliency of a tornado or hurricane survivor to a suicide survivor. Can survivors of such tragedies recover to lead fulfilling lives again?

Final Questions for Discussion / Reflection

Has reading *Life after Suicide* and participating in this discussion group changed or affected your beliefs about suicide? Does discussing social issues or religious concepts "in community" (namely, with others) have value and worth?

Discuss the following quotations:
"People must be given the opportunity to grieve out loud."
— Lady Bird Johnson

"The person who conceals his/her grief finds no remedy for it." — Turkish proverb

"You can turn painful situations around through laughter. If you can find humor in anything — even poverty — you can survive it." — Bill Cosby

"What oxygen is to the lungs, such is hope to the meaning of life." — Emil Brunner

Appendix I

American Association of Suicidology
5221 Wisconsin Avenue, NW
Washington, DC 20015
(202) 237-2280
www.suicidology.org

American Foundation for Suicide Prevention
120 Wall Street, 22nd Floor
New York, NY 10005
(888) 333-2377(AFSP)
www.afsp.org

Suicide Prevention Action Network (SPAN USA)
1025 Vermont Avenue, NW Suite 1066
Washington, DC 20005
(888) 649-1366
www.spanusa.org

Suicide.org
Suicide prevention, awareness, and support
www.suicide.org

The Compassionate Friends
P. O. Box 3696
Oak Brook, IL 60522
(877) 969-0010
www.compassionatefriends.org

National Alliance on Mental Illness (NAMI)
Colonial Place Three
2107 Wilson Blvd., Suite 300
Arlington, VA 22201-3042
(703) 524-7600
www.nami.org

National Institute of Mental Health
6001 Executive Boulevard
Bethesda, MD 20892
(866)615-6464
www.nimh.nih.gov

American Psychiatric Association
(800) 964-2000
www.psych.org

American Psychological Association
(800) 374-2721
www.apa.org

National Hotline 1-800-SUICIDE

National Suicide Prevention Lifeline 1-800-273-TALK

Bibliography

Buechner, Frederick. *Telling Secrets: A Memoir*. Harper Collins, 1991.

Collins, Judy. *Sanity and Grace: A Journey of Suicide, Survival, and Strength*. Penguin Group, 2003.

Fine, Carla. *No Time to Say Goodbye: Surviving the Suicide of a Loved One*. Broadway Books, 1997.

Hewett, John H. *After Suicide*. Westminster John Knox Press, 1980.

Hsu, Albert Y. *Grieving a Suicide*. InterVarsity Press, 2002.

Jamison, Kay Redfield. *An Unquiet Mind: A Memoir of Moods and Madness*. Vintage Books, 1997.

Jamison, Kay Redfield. *Night Falls Fast: Understanding Suicide*. Alfred A. Knopf, 2000.

Lasher, Cynthia Long. *Death is No Stranger: Helping Children Grieve*. CSS Publishing, 2008. (not specific to suicide)

Myers, Michael F and Carla Fine. *Touched by Suicide: Hope and Healing After Loss*. Gotham Books. 2006.

Schneidman, Edwin S. *The Suicidal Mind*. Oxford University Press, 1996.

Schuurman, Donna L & others. *After a Suicide: A Workbook for Grieving Children*. 2001. The Dougy Center, 2001.

Sexton-Jones, Sondra. *When Someone You Loves Completes Suicide*. Centering Corporation, 2006. (small booklet)

Steele, Danielle. *His Bright Light: The Story of Nick Traina*. Dell Publishing, Random House, 1998.

Wroblrdki, Adina. *Suicide of a Child: For Parents whose Child has Completed Suicide*. Centering Corporation, 1984. (small booklet)

Appendix II

Avoiding the Use of Clichés or Euphemisms

Instead of this cliché or euphemism consider the following options:

1. "I know just how you feel."
Better: "I cannot begin to know how you must feel, but I want you to know I share your sadness." Or "I'm so sorry. I'm here for you." Then pause and allow some time for silence.

2. "Don't cry. It's okay." (as you immediately give the person a tissue)
Better: Let them cry. Tears can be therapeutic. Let them know that you're not uncomfortable around tears, but you're there to "walk with them."

   "It's okay to cry. Let it out." (Immediately giving a crying person a tissue can be a hidden message you are uncomfortable with his or her tears. First let the individual know that you are not uncomfortable around sadness before offering tissues.)

3. "If there is anything I can do, just call me."
Better: "I'll call you on Saturday morning. If you can think of something you need, tell me then and I'll do it." THEN FOLLOW THROUGH. As the friend or neighbor you should be the one to take the initiative in making contact. Only offer your help with tasks or chores if you will indeed make the phone call and will follow through with the action of helping. Grieving people usually cannot take the initiative to ask for help. Always give a specific day and time when you will check back. This lets the person know you really are sincere with your offer and not just offering "lip service."

4. "You need to pull yourself together." "You need to be strong for your children (family)."
Better: "You know, sometimes I think it is important parents model how to grieve in front of our children. Sadness and loss are part of life. If you are sad in front of your children, they will learn that grieving is not only normal but okay."

5. "You need to get over this. Life goes on."
Better: "No one will ever know what this has been like for you. How you grieve and how you cope with all the changes his/her death has brought will most likely be a huge learning curve for you. The old saying to take it 'one day at a time' might be good advice right now. Your life will no doubt be different from now on. Do know I'm in your corner."

6. "It was God's will." Or "God needed an angel in heaven."
Better: Most Christians recognize that God is the author and giver of life and would never willingly harm his children. God knows pain himself and God shares our pain. If you ever question whether or not God understands and knows pain, recall God's Son Jesus died as well.
    "I'm sorry. Some things just happen and are so tragic." Or "Some things we just can't make sense of."

7. "God never gives us more than we can handle."
Better: "The image I have of God when bad things happen is of being embraced by God's wide arms of mercy. God knows our hurt and our pain. He lost his child too."

8. "Just be thankful for the time you had with him/her."
Better: "A death by suicide takes all of us by surprise. It seems to me that we always want more time with our loved ones regardless of how or when a person dies."

9. "Time will heal."
Better: "I've heard people say time is the great healer. I think that learning how to make it through each day is a pretty ambitious goal for now, don't you?"

10. "If I were you, I would _____ and _____."
Better: "Since I've never lost someone to suicide before, you don't have to worry about me telling you what you should and should not do. Just know if you ever want to bounce ideas off of me, I'm your guy/girl. I may not have the right answers, but I'll be here for you as a sounding board."

Final "Words of Wisdom":

When you are grasping for what to say around a grieving friend or loved one, be mindful to not discount the person's feelings by using common clichés or euphemisms. If what you are about to say to a grieving friend or family member includes the words "you need," "you should," "or if you just," this might not be appropriate or helpful. Avoid telling someone what to feel and how to grieve. Everyone grieves differently and uniquely. Also, do not put a time restriction on when you think the person should be "moving on." Time restrictions do not promote healthy grieving! Actually they add more pressure and tension on top of the grieving person's full plate. When in doubt of what to say, follow this guideline: **listen more, talk less.** The power of prayer is pretty amazing too!

CPSIA information can be obtained at www.ICGtesting.com
Printed in the USA
LVOW10s1103300514

387939LV00008B/81/P